AD VEN TURES

OF AN APPLE FOUNDER

Ronald G. Wayne

Adventures of an Apple Founder
By Ronald G. Wayne

Published by 512k Entertainment, LLC
25379 Wayne Mills Place #125
Valencia, CA 91355

Edited by: Katherine Johnson, Katherine Johnson Media Enterprises, LLC
Design/Layout by: Jillian Baco, JillianBacoDesigns.com

*****
ISBN-10   0-615-51742-0
ISBN-13   9780615517421
LCCN   2011914305
*****

Adventures of an Apple Founder is an independent publication and has not been authorized, sponsored, or otherwise approved by Apple Inc.

While all possible steps have been taken to ensure that the information included within is accurate, the publisher and author assume no responsibility for any errors or omissions, or for damages resulting from the use of the information contained herein.

Dedication

I gratefully dedicate this book to Josh and Rob.
It would never have happened without
their determination and support.

— *Ron Wayne*

Foreword

Most people don't know that Apple was founded twice, first as a company, then later as a corporation. The first time was on April 1, 1976. Steve Jobs and I decided to form a little partnership with no money, just sort of selling stuff out of the garage. We had decided on the name Apple Computer and Steve went through the steps to form a company, and put an ad in the cheapest newspaper we could find to make it official.

One day Steve came over and said, "I want you to meet this guy, Ron Wayne."

I guess he had met him during his work at Atari, and he felt that Ron would be a good third partner. Steve and I were in our young 20s, and Ron was this, hardcore, political, absolutist, kind of conservative thinking adult. In life, you have a hard personality or a soft one, and he had a very hard, directed one that gives the impression to a young person of "Wow, he knows everything" and "He's been involved in the formation of companies; he has seen how companies work. He's got all these interesting stories, and so many instant answers to everything."

I think it was the first night that Steve and I went over to Ron's apartment in Sunnyvale, he sat down and he typed out this thing that in the end was a total legal document with all the types of words lawyers use like, "The rights, privileges and warranties, etc." I guess he'd been through a lot of them, probably studied every word of them to know them so well. I was very impressed.

So Steve offered Ron 10% of the Apple Computer Company. His thinking was that if Ron had a small part of the company, he can resolve any disputes. If Steve and I owned equal amounts, fifty/fifty, what would we do if we had an argument? That reasoning sounded good to me, so, there's Ron Wayne.

At the time he was sort of like an adult to us and a mentor, and that's how I looked at him. Ron had these incredible talents as an artist. He actually drew that free flowing sketch of Newton under the apple tree that we used for our first logo. He also worked on the Apple I manual, and designed the inventory structure that continued to be used through production of the Apple II. Ron had a broad range of talents, representing a well disciplined life.

Ron ended up playing a huge roll in the early days at Apple before we had funding, before we'd done much of anything. He left for personal reasons, and we were sad to see him go, but we understood. He really was our third partner.

— Steve Wozniak

Steve Wozniak is the author of *iWoz: Computer Geek to Cult Icon: How I Invented the Personal Computer, Co-Founded Apple, and Had Fun Doing It*

W. W. Norton & Company

Available at booksellers everywhere.

Contents

Introduction

I will open with this thought. Even as I was directly encouraged to tell my life's story, I'd always regarded writing autobiographies as the height of arrogance – roughly equal to folks who do crossword puzzles with an ink pen. My friends then went on to tell me that there were people in the world who have a passion for knowing the innermost details of the lives of the rich and famous. That was strike two for me, since I'm certainly not rich, and even though I've often been described as the "unknown founder" of the Apple Computer Company, it was difficult to see myself in the context of someone famous. Then they said that there were people who'd actually be interested in taking the time to learn more about my life and involvement with the origins of Apple. Suddenly I realized the validity of their comments.

It was on that basis that I've created this compilation of my life's experiences. The story of the origins and evolution of Apple has been the subject of numerous books, business news segments and documentaries. In fact, the tale of the company's technical revolution and place in history has been told and retold so often that it hardly needs to be played out again in these pages. This book is specifically for the benefit of those readers who might appreciate the subtler details of my life's recollections. In these recollections, I've tried to cover, as accurately as possible, my feelings and interests throughout the stages of my life. In addition to gaining insight into me as a person, the reader is also granted an up-close view through a time window and a pathway to the world of my youth – and a sense of what it was actually like to grow up during the Great Depression, World War II, and the years thereafter. In short, you may draw from this writing, a distillation of a more than three quarters of a century life span of a man, who for a brief moment in time, was a part of history in the making. Or the reader may simply extract the detailed events that occurred at the very beginning of what would become a modern phenomenon.

PART I
In the Beginning

We cry when we're born, but it's not until we grow up that we realize what we were crying about.

In the late spring of 1934 in Cleveland Ohio, I was thrust onto an unsuspecting world. Essentially, I arrived at the same time as the Dust Bowl, and some of my relatives said they couldn't decide which was worse. Yes, this was the world of the Great Depression. It seemed quite natural to start out with nothing at all since no one else had anything either.

My story really begins in the years before President Franklin D. Roosevelt and the New Deal, long before I was born. Hard times hit my parents, like many others, following the Stock Market Crash of 1929. That was when my father, who'd been born Louis Maxwelton Vinitski, changed his name to Louis Wayne. As I heard the tale, this was done in an effort to stay one jump ahead of the process-servers and creditors.

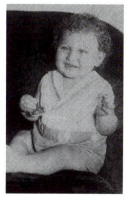

Ron as a young child

This kind of plight was typical of the times. Without the benefit of unemployment compensation, Social Security or other financial safety nets that would have protected them against economic disasters (such as bank failures), people through no fault of their own were suddenly in over their heads financially. Millions of people (including my father) were left with few options and often took unusual measures just to survive in a personally crushing economic environment.

So it was that under this new name, he married my mother, Ethel Bogod. Their delayed honeymoon consisted of going to the movies for a viewing of the very first talking motion picture (starring Al Jolson as *The Jazz Singer*). My brother, Harmon, was born within a year after they wed.

In the vague wisps of dim memory, I sense that my mother ran our two-room apartment most efficiently, while my father worked in the benevolent world of the WPA (Works Projects Administration). The WPA was one of President Roosevelt's answers to the worst depression the country had known since the 1890s. Within this system, my father was one of the millions of construction laborers who worked at anything from road construction to the restoration of the National Parks System, to working for the Tennessee Valley Authority or building the Boulder Dam. It was only through the WPA that his labors could keep a roof over our heads and put food on the table. Without it, we would have been literally living on the streets. My father's employment even got us a second-hand console radio that picked up everything from Toscanini's *Symphony of the Air*, on a Sunday afternoon, to Fannie Brice's *The Baby Snooks Show* and the hilarious absurdities of Jack Benny and Fred Allen.

To give the reader a better sense of that time and place, I will share this anecdote from later in my life, when I was an avid stamp collector. As any serious stamp collector knows, there were stamps issued by the U.S. Post Office in 1930, which were specifically for airmail that was to be carried on the German airship, the Graf Zeppelin. Those stamps are now egregiously expensive, roughly $3,000 per set. This is easily understandable since only a few thousand of the three denominations were ever released. Those denominations were the 65 cents, $1.30 and $2.60. Interestingly enough, these stamps were only available at post offices in New York, Los Angeles and Cleveland, Ohio.

I recall that when mother was in her eighties, I once commented to her, "Mom, you could have bought a complete set of Zeppelins for less than $5.00. Why didn't you?"

Her response was revealing. "Five dollars?" she asked excitedly. "In 1930, $5.00 could feed the family for a week! We weren't thinking about postage stamps!"

One of my fondest childhood memories was of a time when my father came home from work one night and brought me a truly special gift. It was a small wooden wagon, overflowing with colorfully painted wooden blocks, in all shapes and sizes. In today's world, one would have expected that he used some discretionary money to buy me this gift at a toyshop. What the reader might not realize is that in the mid-1930s, there was no such thing as discretionary money. Upon reflection now, the whole array was probably cobbled together from scraps, bits and paint that were left over materials from whatever project he was working on at the time. It was a total delight, as I recall, spending hours piecing together towers, houses and castles out of those simple blocks and shapes. I couldn't have been more than two years old at the time, but it remains one of my most cherished childhood memories.

As I got older, the shadows deepened and darkness replaced the lighter and happier times in my family. My father was a quiet man who was somewhat of a mystery. He was also something of a rolling stone, and had, shall we say, a roving eye. It wasn't until 1936 that my mother discovered that he was actually raising a second family in another town (Elyria, Ohio) under the name of Louis Maxwell. That was the last time I ever saw or heard from my father. Yet if my memory serves correctly, it is possible that I have three or four half brothers who may still be alive under the surname Maxwell.

My mother suddenly found herself as a single parent in the midst of the Great Depression, burdened with the responsibility of supporting and raising two young children. So when I was about eight years old, my mother and I moved in with her parents (my grandparents) in their moderate-sized (and aging) two story home, on 30th and Superior in Cleveland, which had long since converted its front rooms into a simple neighborhood grocery store. Since there wasn't enough room for all three of us, my brother Harmon went off to stay with my favorite aunt and uncle across town, Max and Lil Bogart.

Ron's mother visiting the New York World's Fair, 1939

To expand on my family lineage, my father's family was Hungarian, and my mother's family were Russian Jews. My maternal grandparents were born in Minsk, Russia in the mid-nineteenth century, which was a truly hellish time and place in human history, particularly for Jews. My grandmother's maiden name was Magodov, and my grandfather was Issac Bogod. Their existence was described to me as one of grinding poverty, under the reign of Nicholas II. At that time Jews were one of the lowest levels of society, which made them constantly subject to life-threatening danger. So it was that in 1906, they gathered a few meager possessions and ran, to stay ahead of the Cossacks and so that my grandfather could avoid conscription into the Czar's army – among other threats and dangers.

My grandparents headed east on the Trans-Siberian Railway, or more accurately, underneath the cars of that railway. I recall hearing stories during my youth of that journey through, what they described as an icy hell. They traveled across Asia, and finally crossed over into North America through western Canada. After that they trudged all across the Canadian wilderness and finally entered the United States through Detroit, to then find their way to Cleveland, Ohio, where one of my great-uncles, and other relatives had already firmly acclimated themselves, and could offer some measure of start-up support.

Having learned in advance of the necessity to do so, my grandfather had managed to sew a few Russian 10-Rouble gold pieces into his clothing, and used these treasures to prove the family's self-sufficiency, a proof that was essential if they were to be allowed through the immigration facilities. With the aid of their relatives, Grandma and Grandpa quickly adapted to their strange new environment, and just as quickly gained a tolerable mastery of the English language – although Yiddish remained the household preference. Yet even as they'd firmly accommodated themselves to their new lives, all of their personal and religious traditions remained unshaken. As followers of Orthodox Judaism, the kitchen still maintained the separate sets of dishes – one for meals composed primarily of milk products, and the other set for meat-based dining. Candles and Friday night prayers were a constant ritual, and as would be expected, the front doorway was graced with a mezuzah – a tiny prayer parchment within a small metal case, attached to the doorframe. This symbol was honored by all who entered or left their home. The highlight of each year was when Grandma would spend days preparing the Passover Seder, for the benefit of the whole family to attend. On these occasions, fortunately for me, I was never called upon to recite the "four questions." I'd never been Bar Mitzvahed. My brother, Harmon had and so the task fell to him. Yet while they retained all of their most cherished traditions, they also "Americanized" most diligently, and in time, both grandparents studied, applied and were formally granted U.S. citizenship.

Isaac began to make his living in this country first by selling newspapers at the public square in downtown Cleveland, throughout the heat of summer and even into the blizzards of snowbound winter. Through this grueling labor, he eventually saved enough money to rent (and later buy) a very old house, and a small plot of land in the town of Elyria that was later turned into a typical truck farm of the period. In the last of the nineteenth and early twentieth centuries, there were tens of thousands of independent truck farms throughout the U.S. and in many other countries as well. They were family-owned mini farms, usually only a few acres, on which people raised fruits and vegetables beyond their own immediate needs. The excess was then sold to the public, either through fruit and vegetable stands along the sides of the highways, or trucked to farmer's markets in nearby urban centers (cities and towns). Grandpa's fruits and vegetables were taken by horse cart to be sold at the farmer's market in Cleveland. It was through this enterprise that Isaac saved enough money, and in the late 1920s, he eventually traded his horse cart for a used truck. Then, his Herculean efforts began to pay off, when he finally sold the house in Elyria and bought an old duplex in Cleveland, at 30th and Superior. The front rooms on the ground floor were immediately converted into a modest grocery store, which served as the family business through the end of the war, and decades later. Through grandpa's loving attention, it was this business that helped keep a roof over our heads for the major part of those years.

Since the family grocery store (in the early years of World War II) could
Ron at summer camp, Camp Wise, age 6, back row, last one on right, 1940

not support her employment, my mother began to take odd jobs through the WPA, mostly in garment work. The wages were so trivial that she soon began taking night courses in bookkeeping, and quickly became educated enough to take a job as a comptometer operator in a small office. Long made obsolete by computers, a comptometer was a kind of mechanical printing adding machine used for office record keeping during that era. At night she continued her studies in hopes of becoming a qualified accountant. As World War II began, arms manufacturing plants sprang up in Cleveland like mushrooms. After gaining experience at several varieties of manufacturing, Mama went to work for Cleveland Graphite Bronze assembling engine firewalls for large bomber aircraft. The principle assembly tool for this job was a heavy riveting gun. She held that job for almost a year, until the agony of swollen wrists finally became so intolerable that she appealed to the Manpower Commission for less physically demanding work.

All employment in those days was governmentally regulated, and before someone could leave a job they had first to obtain an

Ron, Ethel (mother) and Harmon (brother), 1990s

"availability ticket" from their current employer, and then ask the Manpower Commission for new employment. Given the physically crippling afflictions she'd suffered, Mama was quickly relocated to the Hickock Electrical Instruments Company, where she worked at gluing pointers (needles) onto electrical meter movements. She continued at that employment through the remaining years of the war.

Growing up during World War II was truly a surreal experience. I can still recall the life and times of those turbulent years, such as the air raid alerts at school when we kids would be jostled down to the cellar until the sirens would sound the all clear. Not that there was ever an actual likelihood of an air raid, particularly as far inland as Cleveland, but the alarms served as a reminder that our country was truly at war. Then there were also the constant reminders of the restrictive nature of a war economy. Every conceivable commodity, for instance, was rationed, from soap to sugar to shoes, under the *blue point system*. Ration books were issued to everyone, in every household, with specifically encoded tickets. Issued by the OPA (Office of Price Administration), these tiny tickets allowed each person specific and limited purchases of the regulated supplies. And unless you had the appropriate ration ticket for an item you wanted, it didn't matter how much money you had, you couldn't buy it. In the blue point system, when you purchased a lesser quantity of a specific item than you were allowed, you would receive dime-sized, blue, fiberboard ration tokens, as change for the difference. And yet, there were still times during 1942 and 1943, when even with the properly coded ticket, there were insufficient supplies of many needed items. They simply were not to be had, unless you wanted to risk arrest or purchasing flawed quality of questionable foods or other products through the black market. All of this was the nature of the times, and virtually everyone was in the same boat – more or less.

Ron, 1942-1943

Though meat and meat products had been relegated to the level of "luxury items," there were serious shortages of all sorts of things that we consider essentials today. Radios and electronic components, gasoline, tires and auto parts, for example, were nearly impossible to obtain, except perhaps as salvage from pre-war stocks and scrap piles. One true essential that everyone suffered was the lack of finding ordinary soap!

While I never felt the affects of rationing personally, I understood that gasoline rationing was particularly egregious to those who were wedded to their cars. If you were lucky enough to have a car (and could keep it in tires), and you happened to be a doctor, policeman or letter carrier, you'd have a "C" sticker on the car's windshield. That "C" sticker would allow you to buy all the gas you wanted. For other kinds of essential employment, a "B" sticker got you eight gallons of gas per week. An "A" sticker meant that you got all the gas you wanted – when the war was over.

Then there was the separate, special rationing category under the *red point system* that applied exclusively to meat and meat products. Red points were dime-sized fiberboard tokens colored in deep brick red. Without these, you couldn't even get a hamburger at a diner. You could, however, add to your cache of red points by rending down the fat from any meat that you were able to buy. You could then turn it in, by the coffee can full, to the local butcher in exchange for these treasured red points. Yet at the same time, virtually any respectable restaurant would always offer a Blue Plate Special (no red points needed). The term *Blue Plate Special* was a carry over from earlier days, when the signature dish of many restaurants would be served on special plates, which usually carried a blue Chinese motif around the rim. During wartime, whether it was baked, fried or sautéed, the Blue Plate Special was always the same: SPAM.

I remember a popular anecdote at the time about the fellow leaving a high-class eatery who was greeted by the headwaiter who said, "How did you find your steak, sir?"

The reply was direct and instructive. "Oh, I just rolled over the potato, and there it was!"

The war years were a time of sacrifice and patience. Long lines to buy anything were the norm. I remember one time in particular. I must have been eight or nine years old. The particular block-long line I was standing in, I thought, would get me into the movies. Instead, I soon discovered (to my dismay) that this line actually ended up at a store that had just received a shipment of cigarettes!

Then finally, as with all wars, the turbulent period ended. It was 1945, and I was 11 years old. Life for me was good. I enjoyed attending school, and after a day filled with the necessities of ABCs, arithmetic and social studies, I spent my free time with the neighborhood clutch of friends. During this time, I also enjoyed a newly discovered fascination with anything mechanical or electrical. My private playtime was mostly filled tinkering with light bulbs, batteries, telegraph keys, and crystal radios.

I can still recall a humorous moment in my much earlier childhood, when I'd seen Mama pull a lamp cord out of the wall, in order to plug in the radio, and I'd wondered to myself, "How does the wall know what's supposed to come out?"

In the latter part of 1945, mother and I relocated from my grandparent's grocery-store/residence, to a two-bedroom, third-floor apartment, that fronted 105th Street at Massey. This is when my brother Harmon left my aunt and uncle's home, and the three of us were a family once again. The main thoroughfare, 105th, was a prominent main street in Cleveland, with electric streetcars that zipped up and down the street during the day and well into the night. I still recall the earliest versions of these public transport vehicles, some of which were actually fitted with coal burning, potbellied stoves inside. Kids like myself loved to put a penny on the streetcar tracks, just to see the sparks fly when the trolley would run over it, and then retrieve the broadly flattened elliptical disc of copper. It was all fun and games until a police officer spotted us, and then shabby kids scampered in all directions.

On the ground floor of our apartment building at the corner was Soloman's Restaurant, famous for its monumentally stuffed corned beef sandwiches. The sandwiches were so jam-packed with meat that you had to squeeze it down tight to get your mouth around it. The only problem was the damned thing was 85 cents! That was a small fortune to a kid with a minuscule allowance, supplemented by collecting pennies found in discarded cigarette wrappers. In those days, two silver dimes would get you a pack of cigarettes out of a vending machine, with the two cents change slipped under the cellophane wrapper. Those sandwiches were truly something else!

Ron in Cleveland, (1946 or 1947)

During my early teen years, on Saturday afternoons, Harmon and I were hustled off to the movies, so that Mama could be left alone to clean the apartment. We were each given a quarter. It covered the 10 cents for our admission into the Crown Theater (the local movie house), and left us 15 cents a piece to get sick on candy, especially when candy bars were a nickel each. A Saturday matinee included two feature length films, a newsreel, a couple of short subjects (most often travel logs), a cartoon or two, and of course, a 15-minute episode of the latest adventure serial, designed to guarantee that you'd return the following week to see how the hero would escape from the flaming car that went over the cliff. Every kid was spellbound on matinee day, and they would line up outside the theater even before the doors opened. Fancier movie palaces had ushers who would dress up in elaborate uniforms with bow ties. That wouldn't have worked at the Crown. On a typical Saturday afternoon, the poor ushers would have been trampled in the rush. The Crown was a theater where the local kids could spend a fanciful afternoon and mostly stay out of trouble. The films of *Flash Gordon* (with Buster Crabbe) were popular movies at the time. It was a wonderful glimpse into the future possibilities of scientific and electronic marvels. They inspired dreams of futuristic wonders such as television, ray guns and space travel. However, futuristic thrillers were always a crowd favorite, like the 1936 film, *Things to Come* by H.G. Wells (of *War of the Worlds* fame), that envisioned an actual landing on the moon – after the year 2036 – a curious misreading of the future by one of the world's great science fiction writers.

Pseudo-science and adventure films were paralleled by the fictionalized stories of the lives of actual men of science such as Ehrlich (Edward G. Robinson) and Louis Pasteur (Paul Muni), and of course, famous inventors like Thomas Edison, first as a youth (Mickey Rooney) and then in full flower (as portrayed by Spencer Tracy). I was easily led by these exciting histories to the fanciful illusion that all one needed to do was build a better mousetrap, and the world would beat a path to your door! How could I know that someone else was already out there building a better mouse?

Reflecting fondly on those memories, I can now see how those experiences shaped my preferences and passions later in life. For instance, a selection called *La Prelude*, by Franz Liszt provided the stimulating music for the *Flash Gordon* films. And still to this day, who can listen to Rossini's *William Tell Overture* without thinking of the Lone Ranger? In fact, most of the radio adventure and mystery programs of my adolescent years were themed by the classics. So as one would expect, I gained a lifelong passion for classical music. Even today, I take every opportunity to listen to and enjoy the themes, melodies and orchestrations of Strauss, Tchaikovsky, Rimsky-Korsakov, Brahms, Mozart, and Beethoven. I'm certain that the soothing classic melodies that served me well in my youth continue to this day to inspire future generations.

As an adventuresome teenager, I had an abundance of free time with my friends. With that treasure trove of time, we would sometimes find ourselves drawn to mischievous adventures. In one instance we sawed off the forward end of a toy, wooden rifle, as the first step to building a crossbow. We wanted it to be just like the ones we saw in the Errol Flynn adventure films set in the Middle Ages. One of us suggested that a leaf from an abandoned car spring would make a nifty bow. The trigger release was easy to make, but we soon discovered that even the heaviest fiber cord was too weak to hold the loaded spring to its fully retracted position. We found that stranded steel cable worked just fine. With two kids standing on the bow, we could finally draw the cable back sufficiently to lock onto the trigger. The completed piece was first fitted with a conventional wooden arrow as a projectile. You might imagine our shock when we pulled the trigger and the arrow simply broke into splintered halves, even before leaving the weapon.

Ron and his mother in Cleveland, 1948

A simple failure like that couldn't stop us and we would not be so easily dissuaded by such a trivial setback. So we diligently proceeded to sharpen the end of a length of quarter-inch steel rod. A paper target was then fixed to the trunk of a small sapling. I drew the short straw out of the bunch and positioned myself about eight feet from the circle pattern. I took very careful aim, and then let it fly! At first, we were all absolutely delighted at the incredible effectiveness of our creation, even though the bolt had hit at nearly an inch below the bull's-eye. Moments later, however, we discovered the true effect of our "toy," when we noticed that two inches of the metal shaft had projected beyond the far side of the narrow trunk. With sheepish resignation, the piece was immediately dismantled, and never saw life again.

Summers in Cleveland during the late 1940s were warm and pleasant, with lots of things for kids to do. Boating in Rockefeller Park was a refreshing treat, when we weren't playing sandlot baseball. Then sometimes we'd cycle out to White City Beach, which fronted Lake Erie, to scamper and swim, or fish off the end of the stone-pile breakwater. There were never any fish to catch, but it was fun to play there. On a few lucky occasions, a local ice cream wholesaler would allow a few of us to sell ice cream bars out of a large wooden box, packed with dry-ice, to the hot and hungry sunbathers on the beach. They sold for ten cents each, with four cents back in my pocket. It was a small fortune in those days, and helped to enhance my Saturday matinee adventures.

It was during this time that my passion for scratch-built model building was born. Harmon, who was nearly five years my senior, was engrossed in flying-model airplanes, some of which were enormous, especially to the sight of a small kid like me. Harmon was so skilled at building these models that during the war, he was actually commissioned to construct solid replicas of various warplanes that were used by the U.S. Navy in Aircraft Spotter Training Courses. His craftsmanship was eventually honored with a U.S. Navy award. Of course, anything that fell off his workbench was legally mine, and was soon turned into a car or a galleon or anything else that took my fancy at the time. Over a span of years, my nurtured skills at model building focused on antique handguns, such as flintlock dueling pistols and Colt's percussion revolvers. My passion for model building even led me to sell a number of these pieces at a couple of antique/gift shops. It was my first attempt at running my own business!

Among my favorite experiences growing up in Cleveland was exploring the grandeur of the Cleveland Art Museum, where I would spend every available hour wandering through the galleries of classic and modern paintings and sculptures. Even more fascinating was their spectacular armory that contained countless examples of medieval weaponry, artifacts and armor, including full, life-size exhibits of horse-mounted knights. As intriguing as these exhibits were, they all faded in the glow of the institution's world-famous gallery of Egyptology. Among the magnificent spread of jewelry, household objects, weapons and monumental statuary, were dozens of displays of mummies, including some that were featured with full-body x-rays. The spectacular mummy cases and sarcophagi also stood out as magnificent exhibits. It was my first actual experience at realizing the concept of time, scaled in thousands of years.

This is how I passed my summers in Cleveland at the end of World War II. And like all summers, they drifted into autumn with its annual aroma of burning leaves, from the sycamore and oak trees that gloried all the residential sectors of the city. The days grew shorter, and the temperatures cooled. Light breezes would drift off Lake Erie, and the butterflies and fireflies would leave. We knew that winter would be coming soon, and we looked, ahead to the many possible adventures of the season.

On a typical winter's day we might visit Rockefeller Park. This park encompassed a shallow creek that bisected the city of Cleveland, north to south, and eventually emptied into the lake. The property was a gift to the city by millionaire oil tycoon John D. Rockefeller. A narrow roadway paralleled the deeply recessed creek that ran the entire length of the trough-like park. At various places, twisting roads wound their way through in a manner that served to link the recessed park roadway to the main thoroughfare which paralleled the park, but on higher ground. In the winter season, accumulations of ice made these connecting linkages far too treacherous for wheeled vehicles, and they were closed to vehicular traffic. One of these areas near my home was dubbed Snake Hill, and next to it was an area known as Camel's Hump. Both spots were known as the perfect sites for winter sledding by the neighborhood kids.

I recall my very first winter excursion to the park, though my brother had visited on several prior occasions. So with our Flexible Flyer sleds in hand, Harmon and I headed off on our great adventure. A heavy layer of new snow covered the ground, shrubbery, and leaf-bare tree limbs under a dull, steel-gray winter sky. As I remember it, a light snow continued to dust the scene throughout the day. My brother (always the prankster) encouraged me to take my first slide directly down the long, two-humped track that led to the creek wall at the bottom. I can still remember how I felt as I spread myself, head first onto my sled, and scanned the fearful course in front of me. It seemed as if I was poised at the peak of Everest as I stared down at the massive drop below. Since honor was at stake, I reluctantly shoved off. The early steep descent quickly gained enough speed for me to climb, and then to clear the first great hump, where I was then launched to a height of what seemed like several feet into the air, on the far side. In a matter of moments, I'd slammed onto the steeper slope on the far side, careening toward the shallower, second hump. Just beyond that second peak, the runners on my sled hit a street curb hidden beneath the snow, which sent me down the remaining 150 feet or so, without the benefit of a sled. I plowed into the snowdrift at the bottom of the run, and sat motionlessly for a moment. When I was finally able to dig myself out of the heavy drift, I stood there like a life-like snowman, and glanced up to the sight of my brother, rolling in fits of hysterical laughter.

Another time, a friend and I went down to the beach at White City to discover what the winter weather had done to the warm, sunny picnic land of sand. It was truly a sight to see. The day was incredibly bright and sunny, and the beach was layered with a thick blanket of smooth, white snow. From the shoreline, the expanding ice sheet that covered the lake had shattered and spiked into jagged, frozen snow-patched peaks, like a scatter of mini mountains. They dotted across the frozen surface that covered the once visible blue-gray water, as far as the eye could see. The temptation to walk out onto the frozen lake was too great for any adventurous boy to resist. Walking among the sharp peaks and walls of jagged ice, it felt like we were exploring another planet. It didn't take long before we started climbing the mini-mountains for the best possible view of the strange icescape. In the bright, streaming sunlight, the snow had moistened into a perfect condition, and snowballs soon began to fly. From behind our protective slabs of ice, mini mountains served as our strategic advantage, as the snowball battle waged for nearly an hour. By then, the sun had drifted low on the horizon, and we finally called a truce and decided to head home. At that moment, a gathering roar of crackling ice seemed to surround us. At first, we stood motionless, frozen with fear, but when the crackling began to roar louder, we turned into two scampering kids, streaking for the shoreline. Then, only a few minutes or so after we'd reached the safety of the snow covered beach, we turned around to see truck-sized slabs of ice suddenly rising to several feet above the plain, amid vertical sheets of blue-gray water. The eruption had occurred just feet from our play spot, which gave us pause to realize the folly of our actions. We determined never again to attempt anything so dangerous and stupid.

All too soon, my fun times and wild adventures in Cleveland came to an abrupt end. Mama had decided the place where she could really make a proper living was New York City. Apparently the lure of the great metropolis had been a secret passion of hers for some time. Whatever the reason, it seemed that now was the time to follow her dreams.

PART II

New York – Life in the Big City

Iremember that warm summer afternoon in 1948, when the Twentieth Century Limited slipped into the two and a half mile tunnel beneath the north end of the island of Manhattan, and finally rested to a screeching halt at one of the many tracks that burrowed beneath Grand Central Station. Aside from the spectacular scenery that had flashed by during that exciting journey, it was my impression of the train itself that moved me. I'd never known that such luxury actually existed, except in the movies. The trip from Cleveland to New York had only taken about five or six hours and was mostly uneventful beyond the excitement of the journey itself. The highlight of the trip, I must admit, was the sumptuous luncheon that we enjoyed in the dining car.

Finally, Mama and I detrained and made our way out onto the bustling streets of New York City. Harmon was not with us on this New York adventure since he'd already joined the Marine Corps to begin a 20-year career in the service. Mama and I immediately checked into a residential hotel on Sixth Avenue near 50th Street at the south end of Central Park. To call our rooms at that hotel an "apartment" would be overly generous. In fact, it was a surprise that when we put the key into the lock that it didn't break a window. The place was so small that even the mice were round-shouldered. This place, which would be our home for the next few months, actually consisted of a single moderately-sized room, with a windowed alcove that was draped with a retractable curtain. This tiny alcove became my private niche. A second, and even smaller niche (also covered with a kind of curtain) contained a shallow efficiency kitchenette. That is to say there was a low refrigerator to one side, with a four-burner stove on top (with no oven), placed directly adjacent to a single tub sink. Simple cupboards were provided overhead and beneath the sink. Outside in the large square hall next to the elevator was a single bath with commode, shower and tub, all shared with three other apartment dwellers. The net result of this kind of apartment life was a continual, maddening dash for the bathroom, particularly in the mornings.

Our first few months in the city were a living wonder and like shameless tourists, we took in every sight. The poor elevator operator in the Empire

State Building, for example, tolerated our presence on countless trips to the observation deck at the 108th floor. Mama and I spent hours on jaunts through Central Park. For just a dime, we could travel to anywhere in the city, on the subways and elevated railways – even to Battery Park at the south end of the island. For a nickel, we could ride the Staten Island Ferry and sail across New York Harbor, right past the Statue of Liberty, and another nickel bought us right back again.

New York during the 1940s was everything you might imagine. Most people don't realize it, but those black-and-white period films were more than just storytelling; they were of the 1930s and 1940s. They are literally living windows to those times and places. The city was a vibrant and bustling metropolis, from Wall Street to Chinatown to Greenwich Village. There were newspaper stands on every other corner, and eateries like the Automat where 35 cents would buy you a cup of great coffee, and piece of your favorite pie. The streets were crowded with people always going somewhere, and doing who-knows-what. Trucks and taxicabs jostled each other for advantage and access along the narrow side streets, although no sane private driver was daring enough to face Manhattan's traffic. The sounds and smells of diverse humanity were everywhere.

Mama found work almost immediately as an office manager with a scrap steel brokerage firm called Realm Steel. This was one of those enterprises that suddenly appeared following World War II and dealt with the monumental accumulations of war surplus materials. Her paycheck netted about $50-$60 per week in those days.

Then, one evening, she and I went for a stroll, to window shop at some of the city's countless stores, and amazingly enough, we came home with our very first television set. She'd paid something under $100 for it (about $800-$900 in today's money). The set was a massive, table-model Zenith with a 12" circular screen. The thing weighed nearly 100 pounds–nothing like the lightweight, flat-screen models today. The set was vacuum tubes, of course, since transistors were still more than a decade into the future, and integrated circuits weren't commercially practical until many years later. When the deliveryman began to set it up, I glimpsed at the innards and was absolutely fascinated! I'd seen a television set at a friend's home back in Cleveland, but had never before had an opportunity to take a really close look at the works. Mama had seen television only once during an excursion to the New York World's Fair in 1939. Now, we owned our first set – as big and monstrous as it was. By then, we were starting to feel more at home and comfortable about our new life in the big city.

By fall, Mama had taken a new job with better pay, which enabled us to move into a larger and more appropriately organized apartment in the small community of Jamaica, Queens, in New York. For my final high school years, I was accepted to the School of Industrial Arts in Manhattan, majoring in Architecture and Industrial Design. Winter travel from Long Island to Manhattan in those days was an experience to remember. Each day I rode the Interborough Rapid Transit subway into the city, where I transferred to the 3rd Avenue Elevated for the short jaunt to a station within a block of the school. This elevated train was one of the first ones built in the late 1870s, and was the last one remaining in the city, until it was finally torn down in the 1950s. My over-developed sense of aesthetics delighted in the tongue-and-groove wooden station buildings, high above the street, with its intricate, stained glass windows, porcelain sign-plates, iron-lace fixtures, and cast iron potbellied stoves. Standing on the snow-shrouded platform, shivering in the icy winds of a cold, gray morning, you could tell when the train was approaching, since the station house, platform, rails, and even the stanchions all shook with telling vibrations.

The endless rows of supporting stanchions, extending up from the pavement of Third Avenue, were positioned at a fair distance apart, leaving a central corridor that was wide enough to accommodate two streetcars and two lanes of motor traffic. There was also a moderately wide parking lane between these supports and the sidewalk curb. This structural arrangement still allowed incidents to happen. One warm spring afternoon I was leaving school for my usual lunch at the Automat, when I noticed a crowd had formed about a block away. Naturally, I had to see what was going on. As I got closer, I was greeted with the strangest sight imaginable. Apparently two of the typically oversized Dodge taxicabs that were so common in New York had attempted to simultaneously pass each other between one of the elevated stanchions, and a cast iron lamppost. They didn't make it. The two cabs were wedged in solid, with the drivers furiously shaking fists at each other from their trapped confinements, while city workers labored to cut them free with torches. Ah, welcome to New York City!

I'd successfully applied to have my concluding high school years (between 1948 and 1953), to be spent at New York's School of Industrial Arts. This was a preeminent technical high school in the city, which offered instruction in virtually every art and art-related discipline. It was my intention to major in the field of Industrial Design. Unfortunately, even with hundreds of successful applicants, there still weren't enough students to fill an Industrial Design class. The school administration decided to combine the classes of Architecture and Industrial Design. This class was conducted under the leadership of Dr. E. T. Mueller, who held his doctorate in Architecture. By way of demonstrating the quality of instruction at this school, Dr. Mueller's experience included a position as a consultant who oversaw the construction of New York's George Washington Bridge.

Dr. Mueller diligently established an instructional balance between his preferred discipline, Architecture, and the appended study into the finer aspects of Industrial Design. One characteristic of that class was unmistakable; above anything else, in his class, *you learned*! Among his other accomplishments, he had developed a finely crafted system of mathematically based perspective drawing. It was a system that was so rational, that even if you couldn't get your head around the math, no one left that class without a practical and solidly based understanding of the true art and structure of perspective drawing. He made this particular element of the course effectively serve as a second function altogether. A pen and ink rendering was mounted in a frame and displayed above the center of the main blackboard. This drawing served as a reminder that no one should ever make any kind of disturbance in his class. It was signed by its creator, Dr. Mueller, and it was a precisely constructed rendering of a morning star. For those who are unfamiliar with medieval weaponry, a morning star is a heavy spiked ball that hangs at the end of a chain – at the end of a stick – at the end of a knight. And this object (the spiked ball itself) had a very specific geometry. It was a twelve faceted ball, and rising perpendicular from the center of each facet was a four-sided spike. Essentially, it was understood that the penance for anyone caught disrupting Dr. Mueller's class would be to generate a mathematically precise recreation of the framed object on display – with proofs. Worse yet, a failure to complete such a penance before the end of the term would result in the automatic failure of the course. In all the years I spent in his classes, I never once witnessed anything that even resembled a disturbance.

In those portions of Dr. Mueller's courses that were devoted to Architecture, we also studied architectural history, framing and detailing, materials characteristics and performance (including structural stress analysis), as well as the philosophy of floor planning, site contour mapping, and an introduction to surveying. Conversely, in the segment on Industrial Design, we began with an introduction to the history of product design and stylization. Again we studied materials, but this time in relation to utilitarian objects like telephones, vehicles, etc. During this course, as we were assigned with designing flashlights, desk lamps or staple removers, we were obliged to model our designs in clay, balsa wood and other materials.

It was during our general instruction on Architecture that Dr. Mueller expressed a concept that had such an effect that I never forgot it.

"The essence of Architecture," he expounded, "is enclosing space for human living."

The thing about this statement, which I found to be so profound, was its inherent universality. I immediately realized the depth of its meaning, in that it applied to every field of creativity with equal force – and not simply Architecture. That is, it was a simple expression of the fact that whatever you move to create – a building, vehicle, a pair of scissors, a sonnet or a piece of music – your effort must be focused on its relationship to *human beings*, or the design and the effort will surely fail.

Yet another aspect of instruction at the School of Industrial Art was no student could spend their first year in their elective study. Instead, during that initiation time, we were each given exposure to the entire spectrum of the arts. We took classes in photography, figure drawing and human anatomy, ceramics and advertising art, including calligraphy, and an entire course on typography (design and formulation of type faces). The purpose (we were told) was to expose students to the many options that were available, so that at the beginning of the following year, we could proceed with our original elective if we wished, or in consequence of an alternate exposure, choose a different field altogether.

The next few years saw the completion of my high school education, and the beginnings of my professional life. The constant need to earn money to support the family meant that a formal college education would be unlikely. Despite this lack of formal education, I remained fascinated with electronics. It stemmed from a general creative passion that had evolved from such childhood experiences as watching film dramatizations of people like Thomas Edison, Alexander Graham Bell, Paul Ehrlich, Louis Pasteur and Ferdinand De Lesseps, who engineered, promoted and eventually built the Suez Canal.

In pursuit of my interest in electronics, I was most fortunate to learn about the U.S. Government Printing Office and their involvement in the publication of instruction manuals for all branches of the military services. I discovered that to keep their costs down, the office sold (and still sells) copies of these manuals to the general public at very reasonable prices. The simplified instruction provided by the appropriate Navy Training Courses thus laid the foundation for my earliest understandings of basic electronic concepts.

As a curious aside, my in-depth review of the government index of publications sometimes led to very amusing finds. In one instance, I found an offering of a pamphlet on the ever-expanding place of women in the modern industrial world. It was titled, *Women, In Labor.* In yet another typographical instance, a leaflet that discussed ground hog meat, was actually titled, *Groundhog Meat.*

My library was further expanded with a copy of the ARRL Manual (American Radio Relay League). This organization had been active since the earliest days of radio (around 1914) and among their hobbyist promotional services, they designed the book for the edification of newly inspired radio amateurs, and have reissued revised editions of the manual for the past 80 years. Inside the pages I found a wealth of background instruction on basic components and circuitry. My education in the world of electronics was vastly expanded, through the work I was doing in my first formal employment. After being graduated from high school, I landed a job with a publications firm in lower Manhattan. It was an organization principally involved with the creation and publication of maintenance, overhaul, operating and service manuals for new military and commercial electronic equipment.

This publications house dealt with many product development suppliers, including a company by the name of Polarad Electronics Corporation, a manufacturer of television studio and military electronics equipment. In my employment as a draftsman, illustrator and technical writer, I was not only called upon to convert hand-scribbled sketches into formal schematic and wiring diagrams, but also to formalize the instructional text that described what the equipment and circuits were used for and how they functioned, as well as maintenance and repair. I was so transfixed by these sketches and information that I decided I had to replicate some of these circuits, and tinker with them in order to gain a proper understanding of this technology. Using whatever sources I could find, I quickly filled my bedroom with wire, components, old radio chassis, meters, tools and test equipment, mostly acquired (very cheaply) through the many technical war surplus stores around the city. What couldn't be found in those stores could readily be ordered by mail through commercial outlets like Allied Radio and Newark Electronics. A cheap source of new audio gear (receivers and amplifiers, as well as various types of test equipment), turned out to be a wonderful kit manufacturer named Heathkit out of Benton Harbor, Michigan which, unfortunately, is now out of business.

Surrounded by an abundance of materials, tools and information, I spent countless hours busily building many of the circuits and sub-circuits that I was exposed to in the office, as well as those made available through the ARRL (American Radio Relay League) Manual. I derived shear pleasure from electronic assembly, and thrilled at my newfound understanding of how components could be assembled into devices with tantalizing functions. On one occasion I even utilized a photosensitive vacuum tube to create a transmitter and receiver set that allowed a human voice to be sent over a light beam!

It was all just tinkering and playtime, of course, but it did provide me with a well-grounded education in the basics of electronics, even without the benefit of a formal instruction. Over time, I'd become a kind of expert, but an expert in the sense of Niels Bohr's definition of the term, as someone who'd made every possible mistake in a very narrow field. (Niels Bohr, for the benefit of those who are unfamiliar with the name was a contemporary and an associate of Albert Einstein.)

Armed with this background of experience and informal knowledge, I eventually went to work for a prominent manufacturer of electronic power supplies, Kepco Laboratories in Flushing, New York. The company is still in business today as a prominent manufacturer of commercial power supplies. My technical education was further expanded to where I could finally label myself as a Design Draftsman. This was largely because my duties at

Kepco reached substantially beyond schematic and wiring diagrams, and onto sheet metal and machined parts design and documentation. It was there that I received a proper introduction into the art of Part Numbering Systems, as well as component identification and inventorying techniques. This was a skill that I would later expand on, and richly apply while working at Atari and other companies years later.

After a couple of years at Kepco, I accepted a job with a company called Lockwood, Kessler and Bartlett, located on the far eastern end of Long Island, near Montauk Point. The company billed themselves as topographical engineers, which simply meant that they did large-area topographical (land contour) mapping for a variety of applications. This engineering facility was equipped to fly over an area in an aircraft that was fitted with cameras to map out an area. These cameras were positioned to photograph wide areas of the ground from a considerable altitude. This photography was also done in a manner that provided overlapping photo imaging so that the same ground was photographed from two different angles. As a result, when these two overlapping images were arranged so each photo was seen in only one eye, it replicated the manner by which human eyes are made to view the world, which is from two different angles at once. These overlapping pictures would yield a stereo (3-D) view of the scanned terrain. When these photos were later positioned in what was called a compilation machine, an operator (who'd been specially selected for exceptional depth perception) could manipulate that machine to draw lines on a plotting chart – lines that each traced along the ground continuously at the same elevation above sea level.

The finished result was a plan that showed the map-reader the precise positioning, shapes and elevations (hills, valleys, troughs and contours) of the land within that field of view. One of the company's biggest clients was the U.S. Coast and Geodetic Surveys, who had contracted them to do a new mapping of large sections of Alaska. A more unusual use of their technology was a contract with New York's Consolidated Edison Company, who operated massive steam-powered electric generators. Aerial photo surveying, followed by a simple means of volumetric computation, enabled the company to determine precisely how much coal was present on any given day in Con Edison's array of enormous open-air, coal storage piles.

Working at Lockwood, Kessler and Bartlett also inspired a real interest in stereo photography. A couple of 127 Baby-Brownie cameras "(at $2.50 each) were soon rigged to trigger simultaneously. This allowed me to take photos of the same scene, from two different points of view at the same time, spaced about five inches apart. That's about the same distance apart as our eyes see the world. I also took the precaution to have the two rolls of film developed at different places, so that I could be certain of mounting the right eye and left eye images properly onto thick, tag board cards. My home-built stereoscope was modeled after the home-entertainment stereopticons that were so popular in middle-class parlors of the late nineteenth century. For weeks, I stereo scoped anything I could find. At one time, I think I had a collection of over a 150 scenes of people, places and events. In short, anything that wasn't faster than I was, got stereo scoped! For more than a year it remained a fascinating hobby.

By early 1956, the novelty of living in the Big Apple began to wane and I grew tired of the city's constant noise, hustle and bustle. Everything was convenient enough, but the summers, particularly the month of August, were excessively hot and muggy. I sometimes wondered what the city of New York must have been like in the late nineteenth century, when the streets were jammed with 250,000 busy horses, yielding their labors (and other by-products). Spring and fall were pleasant enough, but when winter broke, it was a snow and ice-bound mess. There were even times when the snowfall was so thick and the ice-caked roads were so treacherous that even the Long Island Railroad was unable to keep its schedule.

So when Mama suggested around that time that things might be better for us out in California, I delighted in the idea. At the age of 22, I'd finally mastered driving well enough to get my first driver's license. I'd learned how to drive in a rented stick shift, and was soon able to do the three-pedal-gait well enough to pass my driving test without leveling everything on the street. While I'd managed the stick shift effectively enough, I was still determined never again to be without an automatic shift in my car. Then once Mama had received her license, it was off to the showroom to buy our very first new car, a spiffy red-'n'-black 1956 Plymouth coupe – with a push-button transmission. It was only days later that we were on our way, beginning a nearly 3,000-mile, cross-country drive to Los Angeles, California.

PART III
California or Bust

The two happiest days of my life were the day I arrived in New York City and the day I left. Since my earliest years were spent growing up in Cleveland, and then living in New York City for eight years, the 10-day drive cross-country yielded a broader appreciation of our national diversity than I could have ever realized. Mother and I deliberately took a meandering course that took us through the places that we'd previously only read or heard about, or witnessed in theater travel logs. Our adventure began on the New Jersey and Pennsylvania Turnpikes, which yielded my first experience at interstate driving. Then we headed south through West Virginia, Kentucky, and the Tennessee River Valley. I distinctly remember one heart-pounding drive across a long, curving single-lane bridge. Not a single-lane each way: just a *single lane*! As I recall, we simply leaned on the horn and drove straight ahead. For five minutes of shear terror, we lived with the certainty that at any moment something would be coming at us from the other direction – most likely an 18-wheeler. The stars were in our favor that day.

One of the more memorable spots along the trip was a visit to the Mammoth Caves in Kentucky. We delighted in the overwhelming scenery of the vast woodlands, and the aging splendor of the Appalachian Mountains. Then it was only a few days westward to St. Louis and then the Great Plains. Leaving the foothills of the Appalachians far behind us, we found a landscape where a setting sun would stretch our shadows for miles behind us. Arkansas and Oklahoma offered slightly more diverse scenery of rugged farmlands, as well as rolling and jagged hills. Texas was everything that my earlier days of matinee movie watching had promised. The hot, dry, and barren landscapes, yielded everything one would expect of the wild and wooly west, including sand fleas, lizards, prickly-pear cactus, and even rolling, wind-swept sand dunes.

As a city boy, I'd been accustomed to indoor plumbing all of my life. So when we stopped at a crude, roadside eatery in the middle of the desert, it was quite a shock when I asked for the gents and was directed toward an outhouse. I thought I knew all about outhouses, but this was something entirely different. It was an open-topped shed, clumsily nailed to the back of the building without the benefit of a door! There I sat doing my business while staring out over the vast, flat countryside. As if that wasn't trying enough, a scrawny, weather-beaten mule came sauntering by, took a short glance at me, then shook his head and wandered off. I'll never forget that experience. At that moment, any childhood fantasies of becoming a cowboy faded away.

After several more days of driving, the vast flat plains finally yielded to the eastern slopes of the Great Divide. The Wild West opened up as we continued our trek through New Mexico and Arizona, where I gained my first experience driving up and down steep mountains. The roads were mostly single-lane (single-lane each way, that is), but in many spots, road crews hadn't yet discovered the wonders of cut-'n'-fill. The threat of seasickness haunted us during the drive for several miles, but occasionally we'd enjoy the relief of a properly divided highway. In many places the term *landscape* might have more accurately been expressed as *moonscape* to describe such rugged desolation. The driving distance between service stations was at least 50 to 75 miles, under a scorching sun and without the benefit of air-conditioning. Road traffic at times was virtually non-existent. It was this combination of circumstances that encouraged us to hook a large, canvas bag of water onto the fender, where the sweating from driving 50 to 60 miles an hour would tend to evaporate and cool the water bag's contents. We never actually had to drink from this reserve. It was really a psychological comfort against the very real danger of breakdown in such a threatening environment.

Arizona's Meteor Crater, the south rim of the Grand Canyon, and the Boulder Dam offered spectacular sights, which still further expanded the pleasures of our trip. Then once we'd passed the overwhelming panorama of Lake Mead and the dam, we soon arrived in Las Vegas, Nevada. At the time, I could not yet appreciate the extent to which this city would influence my future business and professional life. In the mid-1950s, Vegas did not resemble the so-called "adult Disneyland" of today. There were a dozen or so resort hotels along Las Vegas Boulevard (otherwise known as the strip), including the famous Flamingo, Sands and Desert Inn. Farther out, virtually in the abandoned desert, was the Hacienda. The main intersection along downtown Fremont Street was marked by three hotel casinos: the Golden Nugget, the Fremont and Binion's Horseshoe. Virtually all of them had been there since gambling was legalized in Nevada in 1931. The fourth corner, where the Four Queens now stands, was once a Rexall Drug Store. Several blocks from the end of Fremont Street was the Union Plaza transportation terminal and the Las Vegas and California Clubs. Nearby was the Pioneer and Mint Hotel Casinos, amid half a dozen hole-in-the-wall gaming clubs, like the Bird Cage. Unlike the prominent Las Vegas and California Clubs, most of the smaller places have long since disappeared, including the famous Pioneer Club (though its remarkable multi-story high and neon illuminated iconic cowboy sign remains today). That was Las Vegas in 1956.

Rather than dealing with the round-the-clock noise from downtown, Mama and I chose to stop at the more colorful and character-rich Showboat Hotel and Casino located along the Boulder Highway. This hotel/casino appealed to my sense of fun with its whimsical allusion to nostalgic adventure. The property was built as a larger-than-life, Mississippi river boat fixed to the land, but with its prow jutting deeply into a huge swimming pool. The theme was carried magnificently throughout the hotel's interior, even to service personnel and staff, all suitably costumed to the period. Spending a night at the Showboat was pure luxury. At $18.00 a night, we could enjoy a room, three meals, two drinks and a free game of Bingo. Talk about a travel bargain!

The elaborate design and layout of the hotel wasn't the only thing that caught my eye. I found the slot machines mesmerizing. The wheels of my imagination shifted instantly into high gear. After all, it was a time when these machines were totally mechanical with only peripheral electrics for lighting and the jackpot buzzer, or bell. I quickly found myself fantasizing over the possibilities of designing and building a new generation of *electronic* gaming machines. This illusion would intrigue, tempt and draw me back to Las Vegas many times over the next few decades.

Then, after all too briefly soaking up the lights and sounds of Las Vegas, it was time to finish the final leg of our journey, and in a matter of hours we'd reached the sprawling metropolis of Los Angeles. We then turned at once to establish our first place of residence in Sherman Oaks, California, a quiet little community in the San Fernando Valley, just north of Los Angeles proper. The City of Angels was as prosperous an environment as we could have hoped for, with its thriving aerospace industry, aviation, electronics, military and related technologies – it was a perfect environment for the exercise of my particular skills.

As major metropolitan cities, there were many vast differences between Los Angeles and New York, particularly in topography and architecture. The inescapable difference was in population density. There was a striking comparison of the scattered communities and casual movement of people in L.A., compared with the millions of New Yorkers who crammed onto the tiny island of Manhattan like sardines shoved in a can. Upon my arrival, I learned that L.A. wasn't a city at all, but rather a conglomerate of several towns trying to be one large city. Anaheim, Covina, Pasadena, Torrance, Beverly Hills were just sparse zip codes, as well as those that filled the entire San Fernando Valley. These communities were scattered over hundreds of square miles, with a freeway system spread out like the tentacles of a monstrous squid. Los Angeles was a city where a family without a car couldn't survive, while a family in New York City *with* a car was a rare sight. And even those folks who did have a car in New York considered it a threat to life and limb to attempt to drive in Manhattan.

Los Angeles in the mid-1950s was actually as whimsical as the nostalgic images suggest. Diners with table-mounted jukeboxes, and car hop girls on roller skates who carried the serving tray to your car, and hooked it to the window slot in your door, were common sights. Grauman's Chinese Theater was a popular attraction with its spectacular movie premieres. One might actually have entered a restaurant in the heart of the city, and spotted acting legends like Gary Cooper or Ava Gardner, munching on a sandwich, just like anyone else. Whether it was the environment of the city, or my own enthusiasm, there really was a free-spirited aura to the whole L.A. character that stood in sharp contrast to the permeating "Don't Tread on Me" attitude of the typical New Yorker.

Mama's well-developed business skills helped her find immediate employment at a casual furniture store, while I landed my first job as a design draftsman with a company by the name of Ling Electronics. They were custom fabricators of ultra-high power audio equipment, like oscillators and amplifiers that put out as much as 50,000 watts – definitely not the sort of thing you'd listen to in your living room! These amplifiers were designed to drive huge devices called shaker tables, which were little more than massive loud speakers. Just for fun, employees would play Christmas carols around the holidays out in the parking lot through shaker tables for the benefit of the surrounding neighborhood. The whole character of the plant sometimes took on an eerie appearance, with massive amplifiers built in to metal cabinets that stood three feet wide and seven feet high, with arrays of vacuum tubes the size of three gallon water bottles. The whole scene looked like something out of Dr. Frankenstein's laboratory. The purpose of such elaborate, boisterous systems was to perform vibration testing on various kinds of products to see if they could withstand different decibel ranges. One of Ling's customers was Lockheed, who once mounted a fighter plane to an array of such tables to test its response to high-energy vibration at various frequencies. I was privileged at the time to view one of these tests, which was filmed at a very high rate of speed, and then played back at the conventional 30 frames per second. It was a truly remarkable sight. The entire aircraft shuttered and wobbled like Jell-O as the vibration ripples propagated through every inch of the structure.

I enjoyed working for Ling Electronics as a draftsman. After a few years, I changed positions to a company much closer to home. I chose a position in development work in electronic circuit design with Frebank Company, a facility engaged in the development of sophisticated hydraulic and pneumatic aviation components. They were heavily involved in advanced development work on components that were used on cutting-edge aircraft, such as the X-15 rocket plane. The aircraft broke speed and altitude records in the 1960s, climbing nearly to the outer limits of space, at more than 60 miles above sea level. I was

Patent #3,119,270 1964-2002

fortunate to help create a companion set of pressure switches and high-pressure regulators, along with an exotic automatic fuel tank dump-valve for that aircraft. My work at Frebank eventually led to my first patent, patent

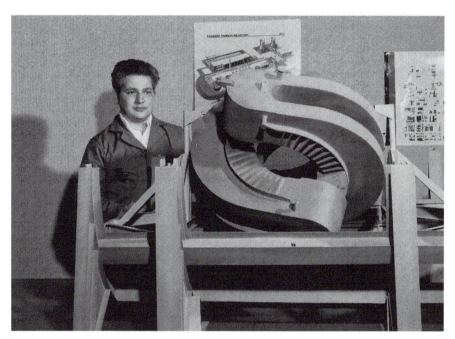

Ron at Lawrence Livermore Laboratories

#3,119,270, for an Adjustable Range Transducer.

The nature of some of the work I'd witnessed and participated in while working at Frebank encouraged me to go back to school to earn my degree. I enrolled in night classes at San Fernando Valley Junior College. While I'd hoped to immediately start classes in entry-level engineering, physics, and chemistry, I learned that my high school credits were not adequate prerequisites. Back at the School of Industrial Arts in New York, I took a full course of art and as many academic courses as I could squeeze in, but the curriculum course load actually left me woefully short of the studies I needed to begin an engineering degree track. My first semester at San Fernando was filled with courses to close the critical gaps. With an overriding ambition to get this prep work out of the way as soon as possible, I decided to carry 11 credits, while simultaneously working a full-time job. I was now obligated to take Advanced English, Algebra and Geometry, and I successfully passed all of my courses with a "B" average. The burden of a huge course load discouraged me from continuing another semester. Eleven units was really an excessively ambitious workload, and the idea of returning to night school never entered my mind again.

At the same time good work at excellent pay was astonishingly easy to find, and within two years, I discovered the benefits of an employment system called a "job shop." Today, most people don't know what an engineering/drafting job shop is (or was). In the late 1950s, with all of the military and commercial development activity that was still available following the end of World War II, larger companies like Lockheed, General Dynamics and Marquard would often secure development contracts that lasted a few months to a few years. These projects might require staffing an engineering, design, and drafting team with a few dozen people or as many as several hundred to complete. These sizeable corporations were often reluctant to hire a staff and acquire all the supporting equipment, knowing in advance that these people would all be fired as soon as the contract ended. It was far simpler to estimate the costs (during the bidding process) if the companies hired temporary help through a job shop, who would then supply all of the needed staff and an array of drawing boards, stools, drafting machines, and related furnishings. As a job shopper, I worked directly for the shop and the shop then would bill the company for my hours. The only downside to these freelance opportunities was the lack of benefits: no holidays, no sick leave, and no insurance! Plus my position was only guaranteed for the duration of the project – I was right back on the unemployment line once the job was finished. It was an arrangement that led shoppers (including myself) to work with our personal tools and equipment stowed in a fishing tackle box, which was often kept on top of the drawing board. Whenever the job ended, it was just a matter of "click the lid," and get to the nearest phone to tell the shops that I was available for work again. The real benefit of this nomadic work style, however, was that it vastly improved my pay rate above captive employment, often with an increase of 60% or more. On occasion, the shop even provided 40-foot trailers, complete with air conditioning (during the summer), trailers that were stationed on the company's property. There was only one rule shoppers were required to follow: we were not allowed to communicate in any way with the regular employees. All work-related communications was done through liaison staff. The reason was obvious. If those regulars ever learned what we were actually being paid to do exactly the same work that they were doing, all of us probably would have been kicked off the property, tarred and feathered on rails.

For the next several years, I was registered with at least six job shops in the Los Angeles area. Many of my contracts lasted for just a few weeks, but some jobs actually ran for several months to a year or more. Over time, I learned a trick of the trade: every time I accepted a new contract with a different job shop, I'd ask for a nominally higher pay rate than I'd received on the previous contracts. In one year alone, I filed almost a dozen W-2s at tax time, and by the end of that year, I'd nearly doubled my pay rate. On top of that, I negotiated a per-diem rate for out-of-town contacts, which covered my travel and living expenses – a perk that few shoppers received. Lesson to all job seekers: you never know what you can get from a client unless you ask!

Most interesting of all, on three separate occasions, something unusual would happen to me during the workweek, usually on a Friday afternoon. My boss would come over to my board and say, "That's it Wayne. You're through."

I remember clearly each time thinking to myself, "Now what the hell did I do?"

In each case, I pondered the question all the way home, only to find my phone ringing off the hook as I walked in the door. It was my boss – the same man who'd just fired me less than an hour earlier – asking when I could come work as a permanent employee. I came to realize that many companies deliberately used the job shops as a source to find reliable permanent help by using contract employees. The job shops, who were well aware of this practice, would place their clients under a non-compete agreement to prevent companies from hiring shoppers for direct employment, until the shop contracts had run at least three or four months.

My final experience in the job shop world was a two-year stint working at Lawrence Livermore Laboratories. I'd been hired at that facility as a draftsman, along with about two-dozen other fellows. When my supervisor discovered that I was a compulsive model builder with an aptitude for design, I was called into the front office. I learned that the lab had previously only engaged outside model shops to fabricate the many display, tactical and analytical models used by the various departments. They advised me that my position as a common draftsman would now shift to model shop manager, with the title of associate engineer. Of course, the *model shop* didn't actually exist, yet. It would be my job to create it.

For the next two years, my employment was as close to perfect as I could have hoped. The division within Lawrence Livermore where I worked was in the process of developing the Mirror Fusion Reactor Project. It was hoped, by the scientific community, that this experiment would eventually lead to the creation of a Nuclear Fusion Power Reactor. Fusion Reactors, unlike the usual Fission engines still in use today, would not require the use of radioactive materials as fuel, but rather generate energy using an isotope called Deuterium (heavy Hydrogen), which could be extracted from sea water. My job, aside from formally organizing the shop, was to fabricate scale models of the massive cylinder, and its internal components that would be used to test this experimental concept.

However, my position as model shop manager ran into a snag. The policy of the lab was not to employ a shopper for more than two years. So at the end of my second year of employment, I was invited to join the company as the permanent model shop manager, with the title of associate engineer. Unfortunately, that's where the glitch arose. When the personnel manager asked to see my college diploma and what degrees I held, I had to inform them that I didn't have any college education at all. That did it. The laboratory, it seemed, was linked to the University of Southern California, and their guidelines required engineers to hold formal degrees. Worse yet, no one could be employed as a manager without also being an engineer. My thriving career at Lawrence Livermore came to an unceremonious end.

Those circumstances led me to fall back on a hobby that I had engaged in for decades: stamp and coin collecting. Over the years, I'd assembled a very worthy holding of collectible stamps and coins. In fact my collection even included a rare, complete set of First Flight Covers bearing all three of the Zeppelin stamp denominations. These envelopes were actually carried on the first commercial flight of the famous Graf Zeppelin! It suddenly occurred to me that this "hobby" could become the basis of a practical and lucrative business venture. I discovered a storefront near my home available for a reasonable rental fee. For the first time in my life, I became a retail shop owner dealing in collector's stamps and coins. The enterprise quickly turned into a fun job, and the shop (named Wayne's Philatelics) soon attracted a significant number of collectors from the surrounding areas. The first six to eight months generated a very limited income, but within a year I was dealing in some very rare and expensive items. In fact, I was soon handling stamps that I'd previously only seen pictures or viewed examples behind glass. My customer base grew steadily and soon reached nearly 100 clients. Through this level of clientele, I was enjoying a very lucrative income.

Business ownership and sales were looking up, until a couple of break-ins yielded a rude awakening. The shop was located in a small business complex, but tucked away in an obscure location that was out of sight of the main street. I was left with no choice but to take all of my coin and bullion items home each evening, and haul them back again the following morning. The increased threat-of-theft burglary, or even a robbery made me nervous enough to keep a pistol at hand constantly. It must be noted that any reasonable person who needed to keep a gun handy at all times must question whether or not (if the situation demanded it) would he actually use it? To be honest, I didn't like the answers that I came up with. So after 18 months, I decided to close the store and continue my business from my home by appointment only, and limited trading to clients who were already on my books, or introduced through other known clients.

By this time, Mama and I had accumulated a strong enough reserve to be able to buy our very first house. We were no longer cave dwellers – we were homeowners at last! It was exciting to have our names on a deed of property and enjoy all of the rituals of homeownership and upkeep for the first time in our lives. We paid $27,000 for that little house (about 1,500 square feet), which included an actual garage, a small porch, a tiny front yard, but an enormous backyard, along with a full compliment of uninvited gophers!

The way those little critters tormented Mama was a crime! For the first time in her life she had room to plant a small vegetable garden, but now she had to contend with those damn little beasts that munched down on the goodies before we ever had a chance to enjoy them. Finally, she had enough of it and waged war against the furry little pests. First, she tried filling and pounding down the holes, but would find the holes either open again, or ones that had popped up in new locations by the next morning. Next, she tried sticking a garden hose down one of the holes, but all that did was flood the yard, while the gophers enjoyed some water sports. It was maddening! The conflict waged on until a friend finally suggested using ammonia to combat the animals. It was quite an experience! Within minutes of pouring a full quart of the liquid down a hole, there were gophers popping up for three blocks in all directions! Problem dissolved.

After "gopher gate" was resolved, Mama decided to spend several months visiting Harmon at his home in El Cajon, California, just east of San Diego. It was a house that he bought while stationed at El Toro Marine Corps Base. This was the first time that I was left alone in my life and I enjoyed it. Around this time, a client introduced me to a young fellow named Scott Bellairs. I had no idea at the time that this 18-year-old kid would remain a lifelong friend, whom I would come to depend upon for plutonic support, protection and comfort during my later retirement years. When I first met Scott, he could have been described as a street kid from all external appearances, but as we know, appearances can be very deceiving. In reality, Scott was destitute, dyslexic, nearly blind in one eye since birth, and was dealing with a congenital learning deficiency. We soon became good friends and I was pleased to support him. In return, Scott took diligent care of all of my household needs, and helped simplify many aspects of my personal affairs. We became each other's family.

As time passed I settled into a comfortable lifestyle and probably would have spent the rest of my days as a successful stamp and coin dealer. As John Lennon so famously said, "Life happens while you're busy making other plans." I suddenly received an unexpected phone call that proved to be a major turning point in my life. The call came from an old job shop buddy who was leaving his position as chief draftsman, and suggested to his bosses at STS Corporation (a division of Ricoh famous for the manufacture of watches and cameras), that I would be a good man to take his place. That was the end of the stamp and coin business, at least for now. Once again, I was back in the world of electronics, drafting, design, and product development.

Over the next few years, I scrambled from one job to the next though I was never unemployed for more than a couple of weeks at a time. Yet my life at that time seemed strangely unfulfilled. It was as if I was constantly searching for something, but I had no idea what that "something" might be. I was about 30 years old, and my energy and sense of adventure were at a peak. I was convinced that my future was bound to the world of electronics and product development. I even acquired a modest personal machine shop built around a new, full-sized Logan lathe, and managed to turn myself into a tolerable machinist, though more of a prototype man. Tinkering and problem solving were a constant source of pleasure for me, and I became so proficient that I was able to transform several concepts into actual patents. I found myself driven to find something of worth that would lead me to a productive life's work. My garage quickly proved inadequate for my work needs, so I hired a contractor to build a 400-square-foot shop in my oversized backyard. Then somewhere, somehow, the passion that had ignited during my cross-country drive rekindled. I became determined to pursue my vision of building some kind of slot machine, if only to prove to myself that I could actually do it. I suppose I should have realized that once I started down that path, it would inevitably grow into an unquenchable passion to build a truly practical, and commercially viable slot machine.

PART IV
Nevada – Boom and Bust

T he conventional slot machine in those days was a totally mechanical contrivance. In its first 50 years of existence, the unconstrained popularity of the slot machines had encouraged the rise of at least a dozen manufacturers. By the 1960s, those companies had produced millions of these devices. The game first came to life in 1895 under the able hands of a bar-supply salesman named Charles Fey in San Francisco, and had changed little over the next few decades, with only subtle refinements to deal with problems of security and reliability. The only truly significant improvement in the psychology of the game came in the mid 1920s with the advent of the Jackpot, and the box that thrillingly dispensed a horde of coins into a waiting tray.

The fundamental mechanism remained the same through the early 1960s. Slot machines were based on a basic mechanism that, in order to yield a profit for its owner employed the standard mathematics of all gaming – dispensing a monetary award for a winning combination at a rate that was slightly less than the actual odds against achieving that combination. To begin play, the gambler would insert a coin and pull the handle. The handle pull provided all of the energy needed to perform all of the game's internal functions. The pull of that handle drew back a spring-loaded timing bar located under the base of the machine that would slowly return to its original resting place, at a speed that was limited by a mechanical clock (much like the one used in an old fashioned telephone dial.) During the play of the game, the pull would immediately kick the reels into a spinning motion. Then under the control of the slowly returning timing bar, the reels would stop in sequence. Once all three reels had stopped, a series of mechanical fingers would sense the display of the symbols that appeared on the pay line. If any winning combination of the symbols were presented on the display (pay line), the sensing mechanism would establish the proper award, and then cause the machine to automatically dispense a drop of the proper number of coins.

The gaming principle was based on a simple concept that lies at the core of all games of chance – a principle that can most easily be demonstrated in the behavior of a pair of dice on a gaming table. Each die, of course, has six sides, so when a pair of dice is thrown, there will be six-times-six (or 36) possible combinations. Only one of these combinations could reveal a twelve, also known as boxcars. Using this illustration there is only one chance in 36, that on any single roll of the dice, a twelve would appear. At the same time, any dice table layout clearly shows that on a one-time bet on twelve, if the twelve would actually come up, the house will happily pay you $30, for each dollar that you bet. Remember, as I've pointed out, the odds against you are actually 35:1. The difference between the house payout, and the actual odds against the player is called the *house take*. The house take pays for the employees, the lights, the rent, and everything else needed to run a casino. How this concept is applied to slot machines will be discussed in greater depth later.

It should be noted that coin-operated chance machines had been in existence long before Fey's invention. The most common of these machines was a device called a cartwheel machine that appeared in almost every bar scene of Western films during the 1930s and 1940s. Most of these machines accommodated nickels, but in the more ambitious saloons, the machines took silver dollars, which were also called cartwheels. This type of machine was an upright console game with a 20-inch diameter wheel that appeared behind the glass in the machine's belly. (Yet another reason why the machine was called a cartwheel.) A row of seven or eight coin slots were designed across the top front of the cabinet, each slot with a different color patch that corresponded to the color of the betting coin. Around the edge of the large central wheel was an array of about 100 pointed notches (sort of like gear teeth) with each notch identified by a color patch. The common color patches were red or black. If a player inserted a coin in the red colored notch, for example, and red was selected in the games play, two coins would drop into the trough at the machine's base. Other colors of coin slots paid out larger returns, since their corresponding color notches appeared less frequently on the wheel's edge. The highest award (forty coins), would be paid for a winning bet on "silver," since the silver notches occurred only twice on the wheel's edge – spaced 180 degrees apart. To play the game, a player would drop coins into the chosen slot/s (colors) he wished to bet on and give the crank handle a short, sharp turn. After several turns on the notched wheel, when it had slowed down sufficiently, an arrow-like clamp would drop onto the top of the wheel to stop and fix the selection. A pointer on this clamp identified the winning color.

These machines, or other similar games, had been around for 30 years or more, before Fey's Liberty Bell machine came into service. The monumental leap in game-play in Fey's new machine achieved three things. First, each of the three reels of the new game exhibited ten possible stop positions, which meant that the possible number of pay line combinations was 10x10x10, or 1,000. This was ten times the number of possibilities that were offered by the earlier cartwheel games. Second, several different combinations of symbols were identified as winners, each paying a different number of coins as an award when any three of the same symbols appeared on the pay line. When any of these combinations would appear on the pay line, each combination would be a winner, even though only one coin was played. Third, and most important of all, was the remarkable expansion in the suspense factor in each play of the game, as the reels stopped in sequence, and the player anxiously hoped to see a winning display. The first symbols used on the Liberty Bell machine were the psychologically loaded playing card devices: spades, clubs, diamonds and hearts. To avoid any risk of violating the playing card tax law, each of these new machines also sported a two-cent Federal Playing Card Tax Stamp inside the glass.

It's unknown whether Fey realized the potential of his invention, but in the decades that followed, the popularity of his nickel-in-the-slot Liberty Bell machine spread like wildfire. The whole concept of slot machines distilled into an aura of character and tradition over time; one I wished to participate in. In addition to the whimsical nature of the game, it also seemed that there was a real potential for making a great deal of money.

By 1970, there were only three major surviving manufacturers in the slot machine race: Mills Music and Novelty (originating from the 1890s), Jennings (who began in the early 1900s) and Pace. These enterprises coexisted with half a dozen or so smaller companies that manufactured what were called Casino Side Games. One of these was an obscure facility named Bally that produced a massive console slot machine that was electromechanical in nature. It was built essentially around the concept of electric relay, or pinball circuitry.

However, the vast majority of machines in service at that time remained the complicated mechanical products of Mills, Jennings and Pace. These machines were purchased by the hundreds, and sometimes by the thousands, to equip all of the casinos, cruise liners and gaming resort hotels around the world. In the pursuit of my new design, it was my plan to retain the relatively simple mechanics of the reels mechanism, but perform all of the remaining functions electronically. These remaining functions included detecting the proper insertion of a coin or coins; driving the reels into motion and sequentially stopping them at random intervals; sensing the symbol-combination that resulted on the pay line (after the reels had stopped), and if a winning combination was displayed dispense the proper number of coins.

While I was developing my slot-machine concepts, I was also working as a design draftsman at a company called Networks Electronics in Chatsworth, California. Networks Electronics was a conglomerate of four product facilities that all shared a common design and drafting facility. I worked in the Motor Speed Control division that was engaged in the development a range of electronic power supplies, invertors and DC-DC converters. The converters ranged in size from tiny boxes to multi-kilowatt three-phase motor drivers, weighing a ton or more. It was here that I established a relationship with two fellows within the Plain-Spherical Bearing Division: Carl Calos and Larry Main. That division also covered a range of specialty bearing products from tiny rod end bearings to monstrous ball-in-socket devices used primarily in large aircraft. As a friendship among us developed, we joined forces in an effort to pursue and launch my new slot-machine concept.

Those readers who've had the opportunity to be involved in creating a new venture can relate to the excitement surrounding the onset of a new project. It's the thrill of starting with nothing but an idea, and then laboring that idea into reality – into something of substance. During the creative process, we turned an insubstantial thought into a workable concept, and then shaped and molded it into an actual product that unfolded before our eyes. This was an experience that came as close to playing God as one could imagine.

Our first machine was a projector-type device that was completed in only a few weeks. Instead of spinning reels, the machine displayed the randomly selected symbols onto a frosted screen. Coins inserted into the model were stacked within a metal tube. When a winning combination occurred, a solenoid activated kicker would repeatedly slice coins, one at a time, from the bottom of the stack depositing them into the coin tray until the full award had been paid. When this first device was finally finished, we spent hours playing it, but quickly realized the general impracticality of the whole scheme.

We found that the alternating flash of the random symbols, which eventually stopped to form the final combination, yielded a curious psychological effect, as if someone were dealing the game in the backroom, and then would come out and say, "Sorry. You lose!"

We also realized that when a winner was actually displayed, we had to stand there during the whole *ka-chunk, ka-chunk, ka-chunk* as the coins were paid out, which led us to wonder, "Who's playing who here?"

In short, what at first had seemed like a great idea quickly revealed itself as a complete dud. There seemed to be no choice but to stay with some kind of conventional-appearing reels mechanism. From this experience it became obvious that while the internal logic could certainly be made to function in an electronic format, the overall functional play of the machine really needed the actual feel of being completely mechanical. In short, the machine should be totally modernized in its internal functions, but retain the aura of a classic character in its feel and play.

We set out to revise our model and come up with a new prototype. In a relatively short amount of time, we completed a reasonable concept model that conformed to our newly refined characteristics. It was then that a very strange thing happened a few days later. Out of nowhere, a fellow came to my door while Carl, Larry and I were working, and hit us with the weirdest proposal we could ever have imagined. I never actually learned how this man (and his associates) became aware of our activities, but he expressed a real interest to see exactly what we'd accomplished in our efforts to build a better slot machine. Collectively, we couldn't see a reason not to show him what we'd done. Within the hour, we provided him with a full-scale demonstration of our machine.

Afterwards, he suddenly blurted out, "How would you guys like to sell the whole business, and if so, how much do ya want for it?"

To be candid, I couldn't believe that we should actually take the fellow seriously. So I whimsically came back with, "As far as I'm concerned, you could have the whole thing for $50,000." Both of my partners chuckled, but neither of them said a word to contravene my comment.

Imagine our astonishment when the man, without hesitation, piped up, "Great. It's a deal then!"

Within an hour and a half, the four of us had worked out a general plan that would relocate our development facility to Las Vegas in a matter of weeks. A statement of agreement was drawn up on the spot, and I was handed a check for $5,000 as an advance, principally to cover our relocation expenses. And then, just like the Cheshire Cat in *Alice in Wonderland*, our mysterious fellow disappeared as quickly as he'd arrived, leaving three astonished partners to ponder the whirlwind experience. Collectively we thought it best to deposit the check and not spend a dime until the funds had actually cleared the bank. The mystery surrounding our genie-like visitor was really driving us nuts. We had to know if this was all for real, or some kind of ill-mannered joke. So to settle the issue as quickly as possible, I instructed the bank to put the check through for collection (an expediting process). The next afternoon, when I called the bank to learn of the status of our deposit, I was told that not only had the check cleared, but that the account it had been drawn against was halfway to seven figures!

I turned to my buddies, who were waiting impatiently alongside, and said with a tone of disbelief, "My God. I think we've sold the company!"

In less than a month, the three of us packed up and relocated to Las Vegas to formally begin creating a production version of the newly named Centaur Slot Machine. The process actually involved us converting what was essentially a concept model, into a production design. We decided on the name Centaur, first because Larry Main was a Sagittarius, but mostly because I thought that the image of a Centaur would make a slick corporate logo. The new facilities included the complete relocation of my personal machine shop, which had been built around the full-sized Logan lathe that I had purchased years earlier. Then while Larry, Carl and I focused on the mechanics of creating a new product, the corporate manager (a retired Air Force General named Vito J. Castellano) and his business associates worked on formalizing the corporation. This involved researching potential customers as well as organizing the details for an IPO (Initial

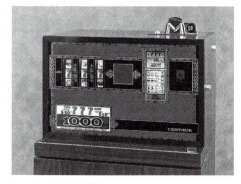

Bar top slot machine

41

Public Offering of Stock). In short, while we brought the concept to reality, Vito and his partners raised enough capital to head into production on a grand scale.

The development work ran reasonably smooth over the next few months allowing us to concentrate our efforts on designing two basic slot machines. The first was a conventional tabletop design, with the general appearance, feel and operation of the competitor's products, including a rather elaborate handle. The second version was essentially a "bar top." This variety was handle-free, and operated immediately, simply and automatically, just by dropping a coin into the coin slot. The idea was to deploy this machine on a bar counter for use by a social drinker. We selected the bar top design for our first release because it would be the most cost effective to put into production. Our financial backers agreed that this unique type of machine would be the easiest to market. The machine's concept was so basic in design that we had little difficulty getting the device formally qualified through the Nevada State Gaming Commission. Production could begin in earnest once adequate funding through the IPO was made available. In fact, the money was raised a lot quicker than my buddies and I thought possible. Within a short time after the formal qualification of our prototype, the launch of the IPO yielded just short of $1 million.

The celebration was short-lived since Carl, Larry and I soon encountered some disturbing events. The situation quickly evolved into a classic example of inventor's naiveté. We (that is to say, I) had blindly jumped into a contractual arrangement without considering the consequences. Nothing in the contract made even the smallest reference to product royalties, our future status within the company, or the inventor's participation in decisions affecting product development. It wasn't long before this total lack of proper attention on my part would lead to serious problems.

Without warning, Vito informed me that I needed to immediately prepare purchase orders for all of the materials needed to build 200 machines. Surprisingly, the materials were not to be delivered to the Vegas facility, but to a fabrication shop in upstate New York. We'd later discovered that Vito had intended to let this New York shop do the actual production run. We also found out that Carl and Larry were to remain in Las Vegas, and I was committed to relocating to New York to oversee the

Ron with Mr. Hussar (shown center) and a craps machine inside the Golden Nugget Hotel & Casino. Ron designed and built the complete electronic logic of the machine.

fabrication activities. It had not been disclosed to us that the reason for this extraordinary change was that Vito and the other corporate executives had a financial interest in the New York facility, and that this contract would be used to bolster that corporation's sagging financial condition. If that wasn't enough, it quickly appeared as though the executive principals had actually bought up our slot machine development ideas as nothing more than window dressing to enable them to float a plausible IPO. What's more, it seemed as if the contract with the New York facility was created around that premise. In short, the entire affair took on the aura of nothing more than a scheme to boost profits by manipulating the publicly traded stock issues of both corporations.

Our suspicions were confirmed when the executives fired us abruptly after they sensed that Larry, Carl and I became wise to what was really going on. We were each given $15,000 in fulfillment of the original contract obligation and unceremoniously shown the door.

Carl and Larry made out quite nicely and adopted the attitude of, "Well, it's been a nice run while it lasted." They could shrug their shoulders, stuff the money in their pockets, and essentially head home. For me however, it was a far more costly matter. When Centaur fired me, I was not allowed to recover anything from the offices. My personal shop tools (including the lathe) and the enormous quantity of components and other personal effects that I essentially loaned to the venture were locked up. Unfortunately, I'd taken no precautions to clarify the status of this material and my tools as being simply a loan when I joined the company. As far as the executives were concerned, they needed my stuff for future projects and were determined to retain all of this property as part of the contract.

I was left with no choice but to bring a lawsuit against Centaur to recover my personal property. After a long, drawn out court battle, I realized that suit was nothing more than a perfect example of an exercise in futility and frustration. My legal council did not properly instruct me on the subtleties of litigation. When the court judgment was made in my favor, and I showed up at the Centaur facility with sheriff's deputies, I only then discovered that no articles of personal property could be retrieved unless they were specifically itemized in the court order. I retrieved my lathe, somewhat the worse for wear, and damned little else. In fact, the total value of everything I recovered was actually less than the filing and attorney fees that I'd paid to pursue the action. I later discovered that Centaur had actually sold the bulk of my personal equipment and effects to another Las Vegas shop. In effect, all that I'd accomplished through my litigation was to become a minor irritant to the Centaur managers by depriving them of a major machine tool and a few other minor artifacts.

Many months later, I happened to be strolling along Fremont Street in downtown Las Vegas when I passed one of the hole-in-the-wall casinoettes. I glanced inside to see isles of counter-like stands, and there to my astonishment were several people playing two-dozen Centaur bar top slots! At that moment, I was filled with mixed emotions. On one hand, I'd endured the loss of a product I created and the less-than-profitable consequences of a nasty court battle, but it seemed, at least for that moment, that Centaur thrived on my loss. Nonetheless, I could still say that I'd succeeded in creating a slot machine design that actually found service in a Las Vegas casino.

As I recall, I was never able to learn what happened to Vito, but I happened to read an article in the *Las Vegas Sun* about a Mr. Sacher, who was the second in command in the Centaur operations (and a person whom I'd come to see in a truly villainous light.) The article discussed his conviction on charges of stock fraud (apparently unrelated to Centaur), and a consequent sentence of several years in federal prison.

This discovery led me to believe, "Well, maybe there is some justice in the world, after all." Life is full of ironic twists of fate.

Now adrift in Las Vegas with a little less than $15,000 in my pocket, I was trying to decide what to do next. Carl had returned to California to open a facility that manufactured and marketed plain spherical bearings – something that mirrored his earlier skills at the Bearing Division at Networks Electronics. Larry had become quite enamored with the gaming industry and quickly landed a position in the Slot Department of the Golden Nugget Hotel and Casino. This proved to be the start of a lifelong profession for him, one that he remains engaged in today.

While I was contemplating my future, some very interesting things were happening. The Sahara Hotel, for example, was outfitting the casino with a completely new spread of slot machines, and was selling all of their old equipment. Over 250 old machines were stacked in a warehouse available to anyone who would pay $50 per machine to haul them away. At almost the same time, I was introduced to a fellow who was in possession of over 300 $20 gold pieces, desperately trying to sell them off at $50 each. Private ownership of gold had recently been made legal again after the Roosevelt Administration banned ownership in the early 1930s.

So there I was, cash stuffed in my pocket and surrounded with spectacular investment opportunities, but I was far too clever to indulge in such foolishness. Instead, it seemed like a better idea to use the money to open my own engineering company, and that's exactly what I did. Within weeks I established a corporation and opened an office on Industrial Road in Las Vegas. To supplement my limited resources, a few friends and relatives sympathized with my ambitious plans by purchasing shares in the new venture.

My first development project created products relating to my most recent patent (#3,727,214) called a Synchronized Stroboscopic Display System. This was a refined (flash-tube) strobe-display projector mechanism, which had the potential for application to a surprising number of truly remarkable products. One of these applications was a system that would project rapidly sequencing alpha numeric lines of text in a device I called a Single Input Alpha Numeric Display. Since this was my first major project, I decided to name the new corporation by its acronym, "SIAND." Unfortunately, while the technical development of the display was uncomplicated, serious marketing issues would have forced me to spend an excessive amount of time and resources before my patent would yield any significant revenue. Revenue would be the key to a successful and on-going operation. That realization led me to shift the application of my new patent to an alternate product concept, one that promised to deliver substantial levels of immediate revenue. This new product was the first actual advancement in analog electric meter movements since the invention of the D'Arsenval electric meter element in the mid-nineteenth century. The D'Arsenval electric meter is the most common pointer type electric meter still in use today. Even though this common meter movement has held its popularity for more than a century, it did so in spite of three specific faults in the manner of its display (measurement) of the value (level) of the electric currents that pass through it. The inherent flaws, which plague the D'Arsenval device, are exhibited as characteristics known as hunt, lag and hysteresis.

The characteristic called "hunt" occurs at the first instant that current is run through the instrument, when the pointer is seen to swing back and forth across the true reading, in slowing oscillations until it finally settles to what appears to be the true value. The term "lag" refers to the fact that every rotational bearing exhibits some level of friction. And in the case of a meter pointer, it is this inherent friction within its bearing that will always prevent that pointer from entirely catching up to the true reading of the current level through the instrument. Moreover, the inevitable lag (as just described) guarantees that as a current level through the meter rises and then falls, the instrument's pointer will always trail the actual increase of the current level, and then as the current level drops off, the pointer will first stall, and then yield a reading that will almost follow the declining current level. This inherent lag in the reading of both increasing and decreasing current levels is called "hysteresis." The true dilemma relating to these inherent flaws is that because of them the conventional D'Arsenval meter almost never yields a truly accurate reading, while at the same time, it encourages the meter user to believe that the indicated value is entirely correct.

United States Patent [19]

Wayne

[11] **3,727,214**

[45] **Apr. 10, 1973**

[54] **SYNCHRONIZED STROBOSCOPIC DISPLAY SYSTEM AND APPARATUS**

[75] Inventor: **Ronald G. Wayne,** Las Vegas, Nev.

[73] Assignee: **Ettie Bogod,** Las Vegas, Nev.

[22] Filed: **Apr. 7, 1972**

[21] Appl. No.: **241,918**

Related U.S. Application Data

[63] Continuation-in-part of Ser. No. 96,566, Dec. 9, 1970, abandoned.

[52] **U.S. Cl.**.............**340/324 R**, 315/129, 324/99 D, 340/378 B
[51] **Int. Cl.**..**G08b 5/38**
[58] **Field of Search**.....................178/30; 340/324 R, 340/378 R, 378 A, 378 B; 315/129; 324/99 D

[56] **References Cited**

UNITED STATES PATENTS

2,510,093	6/1950	Ferguson et al.	340/324 R X
3,036,292	5/1962	Beall	340/324 R X
3,222,666	12/1965	Hallden	340/324 R
3,249,028	5/1966	Higonnet et al.	340/324 R X
3,299,418	1/1967	Treseder	178/30 X
3,366,045	1/1968	Canarutto	340/324 R X
3,400,387	9/1968	Appleton	340/324 R
3,445,838	5/1969	Appleton	340/324 R
3,555,539	1/1971	Richards	340/324 R
3,573,785	4/1971	Miller et al.	178/30 X
3,636,838	1/1972	Chang	340/378 B

Primary Examiner—David L. Trafton
Attorney—Keith D. Beecher

[57] **ABSTRACT**

An improved apparatus is provided for the display of analog information on a readable scale, for the instantaneous display of a variety of alpha-numeric characters and symbols, and for the conversion of analog information into digital data. In one embodiment of the apparatus, the data is stored on a rapidly moving information carrier, such as an endless belt. A synchronizing pulse signal is generated once for each cycle of rotation of the carrier, and this signal triggers the start of a timing interval whose length is controlled by a time delay circuit. The time delay circuit, in turn, responds to an input analog signal, or other variable. At the end of the timing interval, a circuit momentarily fires a light-emitting diode which illuminates the particular character or symbol on the carrier which is positioned in front of the light-emitting diode at the instant of firing. In a second embodiment analog quantities are measured by mounting the light-emitting diode on a movable carrier, such as a disc, which rotates in conjunction with a fixed scale, and by momentarily firing the light-emitting diode at a controlled angular position for each cycle by control circuitry, such as described above.

10 Claims, 10 Drawing Figures

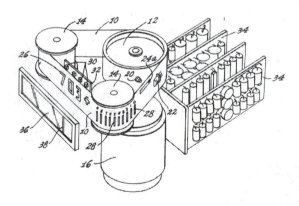

Synchronized Stroboscopic Display System, (Patent #3,727,214)   1964-2002

47

Without getting involved too deeply into the subtleties of the analog meter (that was made possible by application of my patented concept), I will simply state that the core feature of my new meter was in its stroboscopic display of the reading value. The fact that the true reading value was also flashed to the observer at a rate of thirty times per second. This flash rate (which is equal to that of the frame rate of a TV picture) yields a visual imaging that is indistinguishable from an ordinary moving meter pointer. At the same time, since the information (reading) is renewed every thirtieth of a second, the resultant information is an exact reflection of the true current level at any instant in time, and is totally devoid of hunt, lag or hysteresis.

In a remarkably short amount of time, I was able to fabricate a demonstration unit that replicated all of the functions of an ordinary volt-ohm-milliammeter, but with one obvious advantage over every instrument available on the market at the time. Where a typical electric meter exhibits a scale of only two or three inches in length, my meter display included a six inch diameter circle with a functional scale length of nearly 18 inches, or a six to seven fold increase in ease of reading, and ease of interpretation. With my patent in hand and a working model to demonstrate, I immediately contacted every major meter manufacturer in the country, including major companies such as Triplett, Simpson, Hoyt, Phaestron and General Electric. At that point I was totally convinced that this invention would lead to my immediate financial success. I had finally created my "better mousetrap!" What I actually discovered was a serious miscalculation in my understanding of the modern world of invention and U.S. Patent law.

For the benefit of those readers who've never patented an invention, this history may serve as a valuable lesson. In 1855 an inventor named Rollin White was granted a patent that would revolutionize the world of firearms. Samuel Colt had received his patent on the basic revolver mechanism some twenty years before, and during those intervening twenty years, he'd been profoundly successful in developing a small arms empire that survives to this day. From the beginning however, Colt's revolver required the use of loose powder and shot, which had to be loaded into each chamber of the cylinder individually, followed by a greased patch to keep each ball and charge in place. Then, a percussion cap had to be placed on the breach nipple of each chamber, as a means of detonation. As one might expect, of course, there were circumstances when this entire procedure was expected to be carried out, on the back of a galloping horse, while being chased by six Indians.

The unique advantage to the Rollin White patent involved the replacement of the loose powder, shot and cap, with a self contained cartridge – that is, a cartridge where the powder, shot and cap were packaged in a single, self-contained unit. Cartridges had been in use for some decades, but never before, had this improved technology been applied to revolvers.

Of the many claims within Mr. White's patent, only one was of any great significance, particularly in relation to the earlier Colt's patent – the claim which specified that each chamber of the cylinder must be completely bored-through, to allow for insertion of the cartridge from the rear. Later, in 1857, Mr. White successfully negotiated the sale of his patent to a company that, on the strength of this single advantage, would grow to become one of the most successful arms producers in the country, and remains so to the present day, messrs. Smith and Wesson.

It was on the strength of this single patent, and more than that, this single claim in that patent, that Smith and Wesson could outstrip all of their competition. They did so with such effect that the arms empire of Colt couldn't produce a cartridge revolver until 1872. This was when the patent ran out, and incidentally some ten years after the death of Samuel Colt himself. This was an inventor's "success story" of remarkable interest, in that it made the private inventor (Rollin White) a wealthy man, and messrs. Smith and Wesson, into the leaders of their industry.

Of course, that was 1857 – not 1957. The principle difference in the noted hundred years (with regard to the subject of inventions and patents) is that in 1857 there were no "holding companies" or other massively funded industrial entities that could buy their way through the civil courts, and bend the laws to their own advantage.

What's a holding company? (Funny that you should ask.) This question invites another question, "Have you ever heard of General Dynamics? And if so, what do they make?"

Twenty or thirty years ago one might have said airplanes (Convair and Canadair), electronics (Stromberg Carlson), or submarines (Electric Boat Company). In actuality, General Dynamics produces nothing. The only thing that General Dynamics does make is money. They make it as a holding company that owns (or owned) the cited enterprises, and many more besides. In short, their entire business involves the accretion and manipulation of money, through the buying and selling of businesses – big, big businesses.

What does all this have to do with patents, with patent law, and with the status of the independent inventor? To answer that, we'll take a brief look at an independent inventor who lives, for example, in Great Britain. Our example inventor, shall we say, has created and patented a wonderful new widget that would mean a fortune to any automotive producer. We will further assume that this wonderful device is picked up by British Leland, and is immediately put into their production vehicles, but without having properly licensed the patent from our example inventor.

If our inventor had created his innovation in the United States, and the patent was infringed by, let us say, General Motors, he would go directly to his attorney and (at great personal expense) file suit. In Great Britain, however – as with all of Europe and Asia – our abused inventor would instead head for the nearest Constabulary, and there, he'd swear out a "criminal complaint" for patent infringement. Where after, the officers of British Leland would find themselves in a criminal court, answering a criminal charge of patent infringement.

Unlike the rest of the "civilized" world, the experience of the private inventor in the United States, under patent laws that are enforceable only through civil proceedings, is a hazardous adventure in deed.

For instance, an example inventor may take all the right steps to secure to himself (as I had done), the benefits of his invention by obtaining, "A grant of Letters Patent... as issued by the Patent Office of the United States Government."

Then later, a large industrial enterprise may become interested in the device, either because they've been approached by our inventor (or his agent), or have simply discovered the principles of the invention through the *U.S. Patent Gazette*, which publishes the details of every recently granted patent by category. These are issued by the Patent Office at regular intervals and constitute "required reading" by every sizeable manufacturing corporate enterprise in this country. In this instance, our example corporate entity is so impressed by our inventor's creation that they determine to produce and market it at once.

They may even have held modest negotiations with the inventor, during which time they've made some nominal offer of compensation. As is often the case, the offer is so trivial as to be rejected out of hand. At which point, a particularly arrogant manufacturer might confront the inventor quite openly with the comment, "Well, we're going to manufacture this anyway. If you don't like it, you can sue us."

Naturally, having invested an enormous amount of time, creativity, money and effort into his invention, the abused inventor heads instantly to his attorney, where he lays out a good portion of this life's savings, with the instruction, "Sic 'em!"

After all, he has his patent (properly issued) and the presumption that this documented backing by the United States Government should give him an easy win in any court in the land.

Unfortunately as in any civil proceeding, it doesn't quite work out that way – as our private inventor soon learns, to his cost. For a start, the corporate attorneys at the initial hearing point to numerous peripherally related patents (granted earlier to others), which must be enumerated in every issued patent, with the argument that these previous patents "... constitute an area (called prior art) that will demand considerable research by corporate personnel, to determine whether or not our inventor's patent is even valid!"

Naturally, time must be allowed for this effort, and the judge (who himself must deal with a very crowded docket) happily grants an immediate "continuance." And so, our inventor is thus obliged to still further fund his own attorney, so that he can appear in court once again, up to a year or more. Of course, the inventor IS granted (pending the outcome of the final proceeding) a restraining order against his corporate opponent. This is a court order constraining them from producing the invention, or from profiting by it in any way. It is a momentary victory.

A year passes, and they finally arrive in court once more - only to have the corporate attorneys successfully argue for yet another continuance. Based on evidence discovered in the prior patents (as cited), examples of still "more prior art" now demand a more massive investigation than was previously asserted. It soon becomes obvious that the issue of "prior art" will then expand endlessly and geometrically as successively earlier and earlier patent references become exposed - yielding a "continuance" process guaranteed to run for the life of our inventor's patent. In short, the litigation is skillfully maneuvered into an unending process. The fact is, the corporation doesn't care how long it takes, nor how often their legal staff is made to appear in court, since these attorneys are all on regular payroll, whether their arguing this case or not.

Conversely, our inventor must pony-up even greater demands on his ever shrinking resources – proceeding after proceeding – year after year. And all the while, the clock (of his patent, which is only valid for 17 years) is ticking away his potential recovery time. Proceeding follows proceeding, as he's made to witness the shrinking profit potential of his invention.

Finally, so many years have passed, and so much has been drained from his resources, that he's finally worn down to the point of abandoning the effort altogether. Don't think he's seen the end by abandoning this action – not yet. For the very next morning, after he's failed to appear in court for the last scheduled hearing (a hearing that he could no longer afford to pay his attorney to attend), he finds a process-server on his doorstep with a subpoena summoning him to court (and thus requiring new funding of an attorney for even more litigation)! He is now being counter-sued by the corporation for "restraint of trade." His restraining order, which had been issued years before, had stopped the company from realizing enormous profits. And what's more, he'd failed to prove justification for this action in court. The damages they now demand, amount to every dime he's ever had, has, or ever will have!

Enough of the hypothetical. Now the reader is invited to consider an actual, true-life example of this kind of tragedy, directly attributable to our out-of-date patent laws, I refer the reader to the life and affairs of Edwin H. Armstrong, and his decades-long confrontation with David Sarnoff and Sarnoff's communications empire, Radio Corporation of America (RCA).

Armstrong was an early electronics pioneer and a monumental contributor to the development of the broadcast radio industry, starting with his invention of the Regenerative Amplifier. This was an invention that enabled radio receivers to use loud speakers, and thereby ended the need for radio headphones, forever. Later, he created the Superheterodyne tuning system – a technology that made AM radio into a practical media, by enabling larger numbers of stations to be squeezed into the assigned broadcast bandwidth. His greatest achievement was a means to eliminate broadcast static, through his invention (and patenting) of the FM Radio transmission and receiving system. In 1937, supported by the strength of his U.S. Government Patent, he established an East Coast broadcasting station, W2XMN, operating on the FCC-allocated frequency of 42.8 MHz. Moreover, he simultaneously went into the production and marketing of receivers that were tunable to the federally allocated 40-45 MHz band. Owners of his receivers were then equipped to hear his broadcasts, as well as the transmissions of any other FM stations, which had been licensed by him, to broadcast by means of his FM radio transmission system.

This history was unfolding at the same time that David Sarnoff had been laboring to establish his own, monumentally financed production and broadcasting empire, RCA. Sarnoff, however, had other plans for the new FM technology, and at once began proceedings to break the Armstrong FM patent. These litigations went on for decades, with the civil actions weighted heavily in favor of the RCA millions. Still more devious plans were afoot to corrupt the affairs of Armstrong. Not content with his financial advantage over Armstrong, in the litigations then in process, Sarnoff went on (in 1945) to lobby and to politically influence the FCC to shift the FM radio band from 40-45 MHz, up to the present band of 88-108MHz. In an instant, with his broadcasting frequency no longer legal, Armstrong's transmitting stations, as well as his receiver manufacturing operations, were literally swept away. Worse yet, all of the Armstrong receivers, in use by the general public at the time, were then turned into scrap. The 40-45 MHz band was then assigned to support Sarnoff's (RCA's) new television empire – an empire that also utilized Armstrong's FM technology in its audio functions. There was nothing Armstrong could do to stop him, since by then, the patent life had run out. Sarnoff, by the legal manipulation of *delay, delay, delay* had succeeded in circumventing the constraining order that had earlier been applied to RCA, during the litigation process.

Edwin Armstrong went on to spend the rest of his days struggling against RCA, in an effort to secure his place in history as the inventor of FM, as well as to recover the loss of his personal fortune – a loss that had been personally instigated by Sarnoff. Finally, on January 31, 1954, in despair and nearly bankrupt, he threw himself from a tenth floor hotel window. After his death, his wife picked up the torch and continued the process of litigation, until years later when she finally won all of the proceedings against RCA in her husband's memory.

On a philosophical plane, one must ask, to what extent the American economy, and the American people would have benefited, if the patent laws had been more properly structured, and Armstrong had not been driven to suicide? What, for example, might his genius have produced if his time, resources and energies had not been squandered on senseless litigations? In short, in the United States, unlike the rest of the technologically advanced world, if the reader should ever come up with the greatest invention in history, the best thing you could do is simply to lie down with a cold towel on your head, until the feeling passes. The inescapable fact remains, that corporate America (through political contributions, or whatever) has been profoundly successful in constraining modernization of our patent laws – modernization that would bring these laws into line with the rest of the world.

Until then, it remains a fact that corporate America has made the realm of invention in the United States, virtually into the sole property of corporations. This reality stems from the fact that – as in any poker game – whoever goes into the game (or the civil courtroom) with the most money, is virtually certain to win.

In the process, this nation has told its countless independent inventors, in terms that cannot be misunderstood, "Go away. We don't need you. We don't want you. And if you oppose us, we'll crush you." All thanks to corporate dominance over the totally inadequate form of patent law in the United States. These were the facts of the game about which I knew absolutely nothing. Yet I was about to get a formal, and costly education.

With the numerous demonstrable advantages of my new meter over the currently available technology, I felt all I had to do was to wait for the crowd of prospective licensees to besiege me, and then sign with the highest bidder. Instead, out of the dozen or so prospects I had contacted, less than half even bothered to respond. Worse yet, all but one of those who did responded to my solicitation demanded that I immediately sign a Release of Liability – supposedly to absolve them of responsibility, in the unlikely event that one of their employees might prove less than ethical. In short, I was supposed to sign away any rights to litigation, no matter what sleazy games they might play, before they'd even condescend to look at my patent or the demonstration unit.

The one response I did receive was from the president/CEO of Triplett Meters, a division of American Machine and Science, out of Chicago. The gentleman came to my office, and after yielding several hours of deliberate attention to my discussion and demonstration, asked me, "How would you like a job, Mr. Wayne? We'd be pleased to offer you excellent facilities at our offices in Chicago."

I responded rather emphatically that I had my own company in Las Vegas, and I had no interest, either in looking for a job or relocating to Chicago. It seemed like shades of Centaur all over again.

When I pressed further, and advised him that my immediate interest was to find a home for my invention and the patent that it was based on, the gentleman's response clearly demonstrated his actual proposal. "We (Triplett) will happily finance the development of this idea with yourself at the head of the project. Of course, as part of the deal, you'd be expected to sign over your complete interest in the patent and the product." In short, "You give us all rights to this invention, and we in turn, will give you a job – for as long as it lasts."

The negotiations came to an abrupt and immediate end. I realized that I had gambled all of my resources on the successful marketing of this particular invention, and then found myself standing in the middle of a very deep hole. In fact, I'd been so certain of a successful outcome that I'd never given a moment's thought to Plan B.

And yet it seemed that in regards to my efforts at this kind of business, the jests of fate were not quite through. The very next morning, to my astonishment, and without previous solicitation or warning of any kind, the president of TJM Corporation contacted me. That company had apparently been following my engineering and business activities over the years and at that moment decided it was time to approach me. It seemed as though they knew about the several recent contracts that I'd successfully completed, during my short corporate existence, and of the machines that I'd actually completed, with some measure of technical success. One of these was a completely functional, coin-operated craps machine, on which a player could place any bet that could be made on any live table game. There were twenty-four betting options to the game in fact, and better still, the game included the capacity for an *infinite come* – a feature that would impress anyone with a proper understanding of the game of craps. What made this feature remarkable in a technical sense was the fact that to achieve it, meant that the equipment had to be able to "carry on" up to six parallel games of craps, at the same time. Moreover, that machine, after delivery to my customer, was eventually granted certification by the Nevada State Gaming Control Board.

For this particular project, I'd designed and build my own enclosure and reels mechanism, but employed a similar logic circuit that I'd developed earlier for use in equipment, which had already been structured within the facilities of a man named John Hussar (early in 1972). It was equipment that had already been placed in service at the Golden Nugget in downtown Las Vegas, in October of 1972.

An unintended consequence of this new combination of features occurred while I was having the machine qualified by the Nevada State Gaming Control Board. As part of the qualification process, this new machine was put into actual service at the Golden Nugget Casino. The test interval lasted for four weeks and during the testing period, I was responsible for keeping the machine in proper operating condition, 24 hours a day. One service call came in at 3:00 a.m. They needed me to go down to the casino and fix an unusual problem. Upon arriving at the Nugget, I was told that the machine was locked up and it wouldn't accept any more coins. The bets that were already placed on the machine couldn't be played, nor would the command button throw the dice. It only took me a few seconds to discover the nature of the problem. In addition to the fundamentals of the game of craps itself, and all of the options and propositions, it was possible to wager up to 10 coins each betting position. Once a coin was inserted into the machine, no additional coins could be inserted, nor could the dice be thrown until the last coin that was played had been applied to one of the available bets.

When I arrived at the casino with my toolbox in hand, an unhappy and drunk player confronted me. He was so drunk that the casino hands were taking bets to see how long it would take the fellow to keel over. There were 24 kinds of bets that could be played simultaneously on my machine, and up to 10 coins could be wagered on each, and that's exactly what this drunk player had done! He'd inserted 240 quarters into the machine and then dropped in one more coin!

The result was a machine effectively saying, "OK, ya nut. You filled all the bet registers and then put in one more coin, with no place to bet it!"

It was an easy fix for me. I simply got inside the machine, bypassed the lockout and threw the dice. For his 240-coin bet, the fellow "sevened out" and received a payout of 70 coins. It was then that he actually did pass out!

I admit that part of the problem with the lockout was my failure to include one more logic element. That additional element would automatically sense when all of the registers were full and then lock up the coin acceptor, so that no further coins could be inserted. I confess that it never really occurred to me that someone would actually put 240 coins (six rolls of quarters) into the machine on a single play!

After that testing period ended, the machine and another one I designed were both qualified by the Commission and allowed into service. Of course, both of these machines had been built under contract to other companies, so that my total compensation was limited only to the development contract fee. I never received a dime from any copies of the machines that might additionally have been built by my clients based on my designs, and certainly no profits from any street revenue that might have been generated. While I had demonstrated my abilities as a practical engineer magnificently, I also showed that I really had no business "being in business." This reality was further solidified by my failure to successfully market my meter invention.

I had failed to take proper note of a sign that I'd printed out and placed over my office door, which read, "Why work for others for 8 hours a day, when you can go into business for yourself, and work 16 hours a day?" All of this explains my state of mind on that fateful day when the president of TJM Corporation walked into my office.

The name TJM was actually an acronym containing the first letters of Jennings, Mills, and Triner Scale. The latter (Triner Scale) was an older company whose holdings included Keeney Games, a company that had been in the gaming equipment business for some time, and offered a projector type console slot machine. My earlier machine had been a table model, and the Keeney Games machine was a rather massive console product and functioned much like the first machine that Carl, Larry and I had built in the shop behind my house. As I had initially presumed the Keeney machine would never actually achieve anything more than modest success. Mills and Jennings were the industry leaders for many decades by the 1960s. Pace, at that time, was running as a distant third in the competition.

From overseas, there was still another outside enterprise that had come into the game during the preceding decade. It was an enterprise that further added to the business stress of the Mills, Jennings and Pace companies. Because of this stressed business environment, the Pace enterprise was virtually driven into bankruptcy, while the two remaining companies were eventually obliged to come under the corporate umbrella of a single entity – the TJM Corporation. Rather than introducing any form of new technology, this new competitor was a company that began to market a product that was internally structured as a virtual rubberstamp of the commonest design of the Mills machine. That is to say, it was a product constructed with machined-parts, a slot machine mechanism, and a mechanism that seemed indistinguishable from the products that Mills had been building and marketing for nearly the preceding four decades. More curious still, the cast-iron frames of these new, competitive slots even displayed the same foundry component numbers that Mills had employed over the same span of time. This mystery quickly evaporated when they discovered that the new intruder to the industry had actually used the Mills' cast-iron frame components as tooling to press the sand-casting molds for their new product. This wholly new competitor, that seemed to spring up from nowhere, was in fact a company called Sega, out of Japan. The word on the street was that following the war Sega (among their other efforts) had snagged an old Mills slot, out the rubble of a Japanese bar. Over time, they'd simply recreated it, in some instances using the original Mills parts as the basis for their tooling – which explained why the products of those tools carried the same Mills part numbers, as the corresponding parts used in the old Mills machines.

Then an even more threatening situation began to evolve, to the detriment of the old line companies, when some really big money came into the slot machine industry. Rampant rumors soon began to fly that this funding was actually of Mafia origin. There was never any proof, of course, but the rumors spread, nonetheless. Yet whatever the source, that money was being used to reignited an ancient manufacturer of a console-type slot machine (a very large, floor-model machine). That old-line company, who'd been building their machine around electric, pinball technology, was Bally.

Through that corporate shell (Bally) unlimited funds were poured into the design and manufacture of a massive new machine. Curiously, though, this new product seemed to violate all of the standing rules that were understood to govern effective gaming machine design. For instance, in spite of the exceptionally high value of casino floor space, the new Bally machine had a *footprint* (e.g., the counter-top space it consumed) that was at least 25% greater than any other product available. What's more, while the machines from Mills and Jennings were built around the inherent durability of machined-part technology and metal castings, the Bally product was constructed almost entirely of sheet-metal parts and plastic bearings. Also, the logic circuitry of the new system (as had been employed by the parent company, Bally, for several decades), was built around electric-pinball circuitry. Yet the timing that governed all of the game functions still used a mechanical clock, of virtually identical design to all other mechanical machines that were then in use. In spite of all of these technical and human engineering limitations, within a decade Bally had grown to nearly dominate the slot-machine industry.

So how did they do it? Actually, it was quite easy. They simply bought the industry. Until the newly rejuvenated Bally had come along, any large, new hotel casinos under construction would likely go to Mills to try and contract for a 1,000 new machines. Mills would tell the hotel owners that each machine would cost a $1,000, leading the prospective buyer to inquire about terms. Mills' standard response was often (and I paraphrase), "We're a slot machine manufacturer. If you want terms, go to the bank. When you give us a $1 million, you'll get your thousand machines." This would lead the hotel owners to feel snubbed, and in turn they were encouraged to try Jennings as a source for their slot machine needs. Jennings, at the time, was building what was then considered the Cadillac machine of the industry, but their response to the applicant hotel owner was a bit different.

In essence they said, "Give us a $1,250,000 and you'll get your thousand slot machines." (The Jennings machines were about $1,250 each.)

When Bally became a player in the game, the business of buying slot machines changed dramatically. Having been effectively "flipped off" by the older companies, the prospective buyer would approach the new guys on the block. Bally's response, however, was totally different, and one that had never been seen in that market before.

Their answer was, "OK. Give us 5% down, about $75,000, and over the coming week our trucks will start leaving the machines on your dock. After that, we'll take our installment payments as a percentage of the 'drop.'" (That is, a percentage of the winnings of the machines.) This business strategy had been bolstered (it was said) by a $25 million base, making it only a matter of time before Bally effectively owned the slot machine industry. Over time, as already stated, Pace was forced out of business altogether, and Mills and Jennings fell under the ownership of the holding company named TJM Corporation.

Unbeknownst to me, the executives at TJM had apparently been following my engineering and business activities with interest, particularly after the successful licensing of my two gaming machine developments. It seemed that in an effort to retain some kind of foothold in the industry, TJM had made the decision to develop a highly refined slot machine, with some measure of new technology, under the quality shield of the Jennings name. The main shop facilities were located in Chicago and were then engaged in designing a totally new game cabinet and basic reels structure. What they really needed to succeed, and to clinch the market, was a new *electronic* logic to run it all. It was with this idea in mind that I was invited to relocate to TJM's new offices in Reno, Nevada, where I would have access to all the facilities and materials needed to create this new logic, and to adapt it to their new reels systems and cabinet that was under creation in Chicago.

With no other prospects in sight and the very real potential to satisfy my life-long passion, I accepted their offer. It was the midst of a blizzard, and sixteen below zero, when I arrived in Reno in the after dark cold of a January evening. Not a very prepossessing start to my new adventure. After more than 22 years of living through winters in Cleveland and New York, I'd developed a strong opinion about cold temperatures, wind chill and snow. Effectively, if I never saw snow again, it would be too soon. Weather conditions aside, I was excited to embark on yet another remarkable project. The prospect that at last I'd be able to create the kind of machine I always wanted to build was incredibly exhilarating. Better still, I'd have access to all the materials I needed, and all the toys I could play with.

Once more the game was afoot, and the first three or four months with TJM were (to that point) the most exciting of my life. More than the project itself, I was actually working within the aura of a truly old-line slot-machine company, with the potential of my playing a significant role in the evolving history of that well-established enterprise. To be an actual player in such a game seemed at the time to be the height of good fortune. I approached the circuit design project with an entirely new outlook. Over the years, I'd become a master at the design of a type of electronic logic circuit that was almost unique to this industry, and to many others as well. It was an electronic logic system based on a solid-state component called a Silicon Controlled Rectifier. (Don't trouble yourself trying to figure it out. Only someone familiar with the subtleties of solid state electronic components would recognize this device – though even they might not necessarily know how to use them to build logic circuits.)

It took me several months to put the initial working bench model together and to begin a series of carefully programmed testing. As it turned out, I wasn't all that happy with the performance of the first design to come off my drawing board, which was not unusual when creating any new product or circuit. The next stage, as was typical in this kind of work, was the ongoing refinement of the initial design. The executives, it seemed, were so anxious to get the product on the road, that they went ahead and ordered sufficient materials (including reproductions of the initial printed circuit boards) to build 10 prototype machines. They even arranged to schedule the shop crew to physically assemble these prototypes. All of this work was done, as I understood it, to place the completed prototypes on the street, for field test purposes (much as the Gaming Commission would require, during formal product qualification).

Unfortunately, this was when TJM became the victim of a very destructive bit of sabotage apparently at the hands of one of their competitors. While I was involved in the development of the new Jennings machine, the corporate entity (TJM) was still heavily into the production of a decades-old standby Mills design, and had recently received an order from a cruise ship for 300 of these stock Mills machines. These machines were to be delivered to a newly built cruise liner that was then docked at some location along the coast of Florida. However, as the crates with the machines packed inside sat on the docks of a warehouse (or were otherwise in transit) someone had pasted over the original "THIS SIDE UP" markings on each crate. In fact, they had gone so far as to over-paste those markings with identical coverings of the same labels, except that these new paste-over labels had been affixed, upside down! Naturally, the freight handlers, in an effort to correct what they regarded as a handling fault, tried to correct that apparent fault by righting up every case. As a result, when the shipment arrived in Florida and the crates were opened, workers found that every machine had finished its journey, shipped upside down. Worse yet, the constant jostling of freight transport had dropped the unsupported internal mechanisms within each case, onto the unprotected sheet-metal reels. The result was that every reel, inside every machine, was crushed beyond repair.

When executives of TJM learned of the disaster, they conducted an emergency run of replacement parts and dispatched them, together with a crew of men, to the cruise ship's operation offices in Florida. The action was conducted with such urgency that it even included some of the personnel from the Reno facility. It was a race against time to complete all of the repairs before the scheduled sailing time of the ship. The cost to TJM ran into the tens of thousands, or even more.

The Chicago office of TJM was desperate to understand exactly what had happened. The entire functional mechanism in one of those machines was so designed that it could be readily removed by sliding it out of the back of the cabinet along its tracks. At the same time, when installed in the cabinet, those mechanisms were secured to their tracks by latches. Though in any manner of conventional use, those latches should well have kept the mechanisms in place, even upside down, no one could recall a circumstance when that theory had ever been tested. The implication then followed, that in addition to the villains who'd relabeled the crates while in transit, there could well have been someone inside the Mills factory, who might have tampered with locking latches before the equipment was shipped – just to make sure that the sabotage would be most effective.

In consequence of this costly affair, there was a more-than-urgent need for a substantial increase in sales revenue, and supposedly under that motivation I was pressed to complete my production design work as quickly as possible. It also was my understanding that I was to get the ten prototypes upgraded for the street test service as soon as possible, which left me with no time whatsoever to redesign the circuit boards in a manner that would reflect my finalized circuit changes. In short, the rework of the first ten machines was total patchwork.

To aid the reader in a proper understanding of the situation, the first-design of prototype circuits, in a small-shop environment such as that which existed in the TJM Reno office, invariably demands a phase of development called prototype analysis, which immediately follows prototype construction. By way of such analysis, any design errors, concept revisions, or unanticipated circuit conflicts can be properly addressed, in a manner that then leads directly to a finalized production design. Once all such changes are incorporated into the final design, the circuit board (which provides the means for an automatic, rapid and accurate re-creation of the finished circuitry, during the production phase of all of the internal logic wiring) can be properly upgraded, and released for production. In short, prototypes are the learning devices of any new design, from which finalized or production designs, can then be created. Yet, in conflict with this well understood procedure, I was suddenly told that the ten prototypes were not to be put into a controlled field test after all. Instead, to my astonishment I was informed that *these prototype machines had already been sold.*

Reno Management had decided to actually sell machines that had never been intended for formal service, except as experimental equipment. Without any fieldtesting or serious post-prototype analysis, it was certain that the buyers would experience disastrous street performance. I was flabbergasted to realize that the management of TJM (as the producers of so-called "Cadillac" products) would actually sell untested equipment, seriously jeopardizing the Jennings name and company credibility. I must admit at this point, I was so furious at such an outrageous business decision that I warned Reno management that if they actually shipped that equipment, as being serviceable products, I would resign. My initial hope was that such a threat would properly convey my concerns for the Jennings reputation, and get them to understand the risk they were undertaking to the company's reputation. Then too, there was also some measure of concern in regards to my own reputation. After all, the last thing I needed was to be known in the industry as the engineer who'd been responsible for bringing down the Jennings name. I actually believed that in the face of my threat they'd come to reason, and at least delay shipment of the product for six to eight weeks. That would allow me time to amply check the product's reliability before it went out the door. Instead, executives went ahead and shipped those machines to the client, and I promptly resigned (in a state of absolute amazement).

I tried to make sense of the whole TJM affair for weeks, until I recalled a fleeting memory. It came back to me that the Managing Director of TJM's Reno offices had been hired only six months before I joined the company. The manager's previous experience was principally gained through his employment at Bally. Without proof of any kind, the whole crate mishap, coupled with a seemingly irrational corporate business judgment seemed (at least on the surface) to explain everything.

My fanciful dream – my passion of designing and building a better line of products in the field of slot machines – was now lost in a grubby battleground of corporate dirty tricks and greed. I decided it was time for me to get out of this sleazy world of backroom deals and smoke and mirrors, and back to a working environment where all I had to do was push a pencil and draw a paycheck. In a matter of weeks, I returned to Los Angeles with $600 in borrowed money. After the loss of my company, SIAND, I was determined to buy back all of the stock that a generous circle of family and friends had bought to get the company off the ground. Even before I left Las Vegas, every creditor was paid off, 100 cents on the dollar. I was literally left with nothing.

People questioned my concern over repaying my stockholders arguing, "That's what a corporate shell was for, to limit personal liability, in the event of a failed enterprise." I just didn't see it that way. The business failure was my responsibility and I wasn't going to have people lose money because of my inability to make the business succeed. It took nearly two years, but over time, I actually did buy back every share of stock. And when it was done, I could look into a mirror without grimacing.

PART V
California – The Return

I simply decided to return to Los Angeles to the home Mama had kept since leaving her stay with Harmon. This home would serve as my base, so I could begin earning a respectable living and generate some income once again. The return to my old world of job shopping was a real comfort, as were the job shop managers who welcomed me back with open arms. My timing was perfect for the one shop that served as my principal employer. An aerospace facility, called Librascope, was putting together a new team and my new boss thought I'd make a perfect lead man in the Senior Design Group. As generous as the offer sounded, I had to graciously decline. The past year's drama had taken everything out of me emotionally, physically, and psychologically. I was in desperate need of a break from any kind of responsibility. I told the shop manager that he could expect me to put in 10 hours of work on any eight-hour day, but when 5 p.m. rolled around, my pencil would be standing on end, and I'd be out the door. At that point, I was the epitome of an emotional wreck.

During the early part of 1973, I gradually began to recover my confidence and functional strength. It was then that I determined to salve my shredded nerves by undertaking the construction of the most ambitious model I'd ever attempted. I happened to run into a fellow who'd been running some sort of video monitoring business (the exact nature I was never clear on). At any rate, he was in the process of replacing his entire inventory of Sony reel-to-reel video tape recorder sets. (Remember these were the days before VCRs.) Each set consisted of a standard Sony table-model TV receiver that had been custom linked to a 1" reel-to-reel tape recording and play-back deck. A video camera and tripod came with the package – all for $750. Despite the fact the system took an 8" diameter reel of 1" Ampex recording tape (at $25 each) to record a single hour of programming, I couldn't resist.

Almost as soon as I had set up the equipment in my new apartment (I was now living in an apartment in Mountain View, California, just a few miles away from Mama so I could spend some time living on my own and recouping after the psychological blow I suffered), I was able to record the Disney production of *Twenty Thousand Leagues Under the Sea* off the television. This film totally intrigued me, particularly with its fascinating representation of Jules Verne's Nautilus. I decided that building a model of that Nautilus would be a perfect project for my psychological rehabilitation, and started construction immediately. I built the replica craft on a scale that yielded a six-foot long representation of this mythical ship. Using balsa wood and cardboard, I reproduced every intricate detail of the Disney Studio's design. The detailing included intricate replication of all of the interiors that were externally visible, such as the Wheel House, the Chart Room, and of course, the Grand Salon. Micro-miniature lighting further enhanced visibility of these interior representations. Two longitudinal brass rods that ran along the underside of the craft provided the electrical contacts for all of the interior lighting. These rods were positioned to make electrical contact with a six-volt power source, when the finished model rested on a heavy Dry-Dock scaffolding. In turn, these conductors were wired to a model of an Engineering Shed, which invisibly housed a six-volt transformer. The intricate detail that compromised this replication included the typical foliated ironwork that was popular in the construction of ships and engines of the late nineteenth century.

I must have been about half way through the construction before a serious question popped into my head, "When I finished this ship, what the hell was I going to do with the thing?"

The process of building gave me immense pleasure, comfort and personal satisfaction, but it still begged the question. When I shared my concern with some friends, one of them suggested, "Why not offer it to the Maritime Museum in San Francisco?"

That seemed like a great idea, so I immediately contacted their curator. Apparently, it seemed, everyone had the same idea. He told me that they regularly rejected up to 50 offers of donated ship models every month. If not, he said, they'd be up to their armpits in model ships. However, he reconciled that a massive model of Jules Verne's Nautilus was so unusual that they would abandon their standard policy and accept my work.

Nearly eight months later, I finally completed the enterprise and made the six-hour drive up the coast from Los Angeles to San Francisco. The museum was located near the bay, at the foot of Polk Street. The curators were overwhelmed with projects at that time, but they promised to display the Nautilus in conjunction with a real life, soon-to-be-delivered submarine, the USS Pampanito. That vessel was a gift from the U.S. Navy and would be placed on permanent display near the museum's main building. Upon my donation, the museum issued me a letter of valuation, which netted me a $1,700 deduction on my federal tax return for that year. Over the years, several friends and visitors who visited the museum to see my replica were told that the model was no longer on display, and had been relocated to a storeroom. I found out the Nautilus was only available for viewing if someone requested permission of the curator. While I was unhappy that my efforts had been consigned to a back room, the model was now the museum's property, and their right to do as they pleased.

That exercise in model building as a means of emotional rehabilitation worked magnificently. Through that project, and the salving influence of time, I'd truly regained my old self-confidence. I realized that I grew tired of the uncertainties of job shop employment and longed to find something a bit more permanent, even at a slightly reduced income. A friend suggested that I contact a headhunter to help find a new job. I was reluctant at first to take the suggestion, rebelling at the idea of paying someone to find me a job. Then I learned these headhunting agencies required the employer to pay the fee to find professionals. I contacted one agency and in a surprisingly short time, I found myself in the offices of Atari in Los Gatos, California.

It was the fall of 1973. After a very brief interview with Al Alcorn, the corporation's chief engineer, he added the most curious comment I'd ever experienced during a job interview. "I've only one question for you. There's one light bulb, and two switches. Show me the circuit that will let me use either switch to turn the bulb on or off."

My first response was, "You've gotta be kidding!"

His comeback was direct. "No, just show me the circuit and you're hired."

I found it strange that Al would base my hiring on whether I knew anything about logic circuits, but regardless of the reasoning, I sketched the answer in less than a minute, and was promptly hired. Just when I thought the job interview was over, and I was confident that the position was mine, the founder, guiding light and genius behind Atari walked in.

Nolan Bushnell had apparently read my resume, and considered it appropriate to interrupt our interview and ask one more question, "Are you a spy for Bally?"

Of all the questions he could have asked, this one caught me off guard.

It was so out of the blue that all I could do was laugh. He left the room wearing a broad grin, obviously taking my laughter as a "no." It would be more than a year down the road before I'd learned the meaning behind his question. At that point I knew that my employment at Atari was truly assured. I was now Atari employee number 395 as stated on my badge.

I found Nolan to be one of the most intriguing personalities I'd ever met. As the creator of Pong, he had constructed an empire around a coin-operated version of that video game. The name of the company itself (Atari) was taken from a key term used in a board game that had been invented in China some 4,000 years ago. This game, called "Go," was imported into Japan around the 10th century, and today is the national game of the country. It is a highly tactical game, which is played by placing stones (either white or black to identify each player) on the intersections of grid lines. The Go board is arranged with a grid of 19 vertical and 19 horizontal lines, and during the game the players alternately place stones at the line's intersections. Once the stones are placed, they never move during a game, except to be removed as captives. The object of the game is to dominate territorial segments of the board by surrounding them through highly strategic conflict. When one player succeeds in threatening to capture an opponent's stone or stones (in a situation where a single stone placement completes the capture) the opposing player is required to call "Atari," just like Chess when a player would call "check" to warn their opponent of impending "checkmate." The fundamentals of the game could be learned in just 10 minutes, but a serious player could spend a lifetime trying to master it.

Nolan was a past master at the game of Go, and so it seemed appropriate that he would adopted the tactical term, Atari, as the name of his brilliantly conceived enterprise. Somehow, Nolan discovered that I was a Go player as well. As the captain of his corporate ship, Nolan would often call design and/or management teams into his office for a pep talk. One day, when I'd arrived ahead of the others, he invited me to play a round of Go on a board set that he'd always kept on his desk. By this time, I had little opportunity to play the game after learning it at Networks, so I couldn't resist. Right away, Nolan guessed my limited ability at the game, and gave me a 20 stone handicap before we started so I could place the stones wherever I wanted. Then, when we were about a dozen stones into the game, the rest of the team showed up for the meeting, and Nolan began his soliloquy. It was fascinating to watch, as he continued his monologue for the next 20 minutes – uninterrupted and simultaneously placing move after move to occupy or dominate virtually every point on the board. While I was getting skunked, Nolan rattled off business commentaries and other internal company news. At some point during his speech, I recall (since the country was in middle of the Cold War at the time) he made a fascinating comment that reflected the level of U.S. technology at that time. He said Atari was using technology in their video games that the Russians could only wish they could use in their military weapons. I certainly learned some lessons in the game that day.

It was Nolan's strategy skills that enabled him to lead Atari as a dominant player in the world of coin-operated amusement equipment, and successfully revised the whole concept of game production, marketing and distribution. For example, it was typical that a game manufacturer would only have a single distributor in a city to market their products. Nolan had an associate (a pseudo competitor) named Joe Keenan, who ran a similar coin-operated video game business under the name Kee Games. Kee Games was supposedly a separate enterprise and had its distributor outlets located in the same cities where Atari marketed through its distributors. It was a little known fact that Atari had been operating a secret research and development facility amid the tall pine forests of Grass Valley, California, where all sorts of new and experimental games were brought to life. In reality, this "secret" facility was the worst kept secret in the business. What was less well known was the fact that the games created at Grass Valley were meticulously divided between Atari and Kee Games. In time, this "secret" became the subject of industry gossip.

One of the truly brilliant business strategies of Atari management was to encourage creativity by allowing every employee an opportunity to express and pitch new ideas, no matter their formal job title. If someone had an idea for a new and interesting game, for example, management would turn them loose in the shop to see what developed. A lot of these schemes were real turkeys, of course, but every once in a while, a true winner came out of this practice. Those successes more than covered the cost of all the ideas that didn't make it. Nolan and Al were prime motivators behind this philosophy, not only in terms of new game ideas, but also in regards to any innovations that would improve efficiency and/or plant operations.

Al was the quintessential chief engineer. He was brilliant, extremely knowledgeable, and a master analyst of human character. More than that, he understood how to get the most out of his employees and resources. He would never define his subordinates by the "little boxes" next to their formal job titles, but instead would tap into a person's best capabilities. When he saw that someone had a special capability or aptitude, Al would give the employee free reign to pursue it. Over the years that I worked for him, there were several times when this latitude of "resource application" allowed me to pursue fascinating and highly productive activities that I was passionate about.

While my official job title remained chief draftsman, I also worked as a product design coordinator, where I was responsible for designing the game cabinets and detailing their structural components. I didn't deal with cabinet graphics – a highly specialized skill. That intricate design skill was left in the hands of the most creative graphic artists I've ever worked with – two young Asian Americans named Regan Cheng and Pete Takaichi. The three of us soon developed a close productive working relationship, which lasted throughout my years at Atari.

While Atari had been in business for years before I joined the ranks, they'd still fallen victim to one of the most common and destructive mistakes of start-up corporations – especially for corporations organized around highly innovative products. As any creative person will tell you, brilliant creators of new products are universally driven (that is, emotionally driven) by the need to get their designs formalized and into production as quickly as possible. As a result, all of their immediate energy and intellectual focus is directed towards the final product, and such trivial details like creating a proper drawing number system are simply an irritating nuisance to be casually structured with the minimal effort and expense. For example, the initial solution to something as mundane as a "drawing number system" was easy – just start by drawing number one, and go from there! The builders of innovative empires rarely realize that documentation systems must be precisely structured to yield the most efficient means to store every detail of information, and enable the most efficient retrieval of such data. When it came to a flawed beginning, Atari's documentation system was in a similar situation.

When I brought my concerns to the attention his response was truly surprising, "You're the chief draftsman. If you don't like the system, change it!"

By this point in my career, I'd had many years of experience in a Drafting Room environment, but this was the first time in my life that a boss had told me (when I was actually the new kid on the block) that if I didn't like the system, I should go ahead and change it!

Armed with the freedom to make my own marching orders, it actually took relatively little time to restructure the drawing number system, and issue a documented explanation of the theory and usage throughout the plant. Within days of resolving that problem, a truly monstrous "systems dragon" reared its head. I was working on the design and detailing of my first game enclosure when I needed specific cabinet hardware. Assuming Atari had some kind of organized method in place to find these components, I went to Regan to ask about their system for documenting hardware – screws, nuts, latches, etc. When he showed me what the designers had been using, I almost lost my upper set.

He said something to the effect of, "Oh, just go to the parts book. Then look through all the listings until you find the part you're looking for. Then just use the number right next to it in the book. If you can't find the part you need, just take the next number on the list, and write in your own description."

I couldn't believe what Regan was telling me, and the sight of what he showed me as the company's parts listing book was enough to make me lose my breakfast! There were countless pages where the successive lines were numbered, starting with number one, and then proceeded into the thousands. Machine screws, wood screws, washers, springs, locks, knobs, electronic components and who knows what else were all jumbled together with no way to find anything and no specific descriptions! Since there were no definite descriptions of the parts, and they were listed in random order, I deduced that they could have six different parts with the same number, and six different numbers for any particular part!

I asked Regan how long this "system" had been in place, and he said, "Since the beginning I guess." He suggested, "If you really want to find a particular bit of hardware for your project, the best thing to do is to go into stores, and check the inventory for whatever might be on hand."

In a fit of complete frustration, that's exactly what I did. My actual comment was, "What a ball of snakes!"

That was when I sheepishly went back to Al's office, but this time very apprehensively. I had to tell him what I found and how ill conceived and costly the system was to the company. To be candid, I fully expected to have my head handed to me as when I walked into his office and laid out the facts. To my astonishment, he listened with great patience as I outlined my observations, and suggested what needed to be done.

"I've been through your storeroom, and reviewed your inventory of hardware and purchased components," I told him, "and what I saw was $500,000 in materials that might just as well be in concrete. No one would ever find a tenth of what they're looking in that room."

I pointed out that just having an endless list of random parts, without proper descriptions, simply encouraged "busy people" to take a new number, and then scribble out some random description. I'd found as many as a dozen bins with different part numbers that all contained varying quantities of the same parts. Some bins held mixed amounts of slightly different parts (such as washers, for example), but all of them were identified with the same part number. In a word, I said, "It's a flaming disaster! We've got to do something about it?"

Al's comeback was simple, calm and characteristic. "Not we. You. If it's not right, then tear it down and put it back together again, the right way."

Once again, I received a formal introduction to Atari's corporate philosophy when it came to tapping the unique capabilities of its employees. I had my instructions and essentially, carte blanche orders to proceed. Over the next few weeks, I succeeded in restructuring the drawing number and data filing system, and establishing a new drawing numbering structure to make it easier to identify all of the drawings relating to the same product. That same numbering system was also used to distinguish the kind of drawing, e.g., an Assembly Drawing, Detail Drawing, Schematic Diagram, etc. I also devised a single drawing number document that identified every drawing and component needed to build any machine that the company had produced.

It took me another six months to create a complete "Purchased Parts Numbering System" and its companion data catalogue. This new system reflected a distinction between fabricated parts (for items with designs that were specified by Atari), and purchased parts (for items whose design was controlled by the seller/manufacturer). After identifying the specific group placement, the "Purchased Parts" were catalogued under a unique numbering system that was so specific, it was impossible to have more than one number assigned to any unique part. The master catalog of Fabricated Parts (consisting of several hundred pages) was structured to perform many functions, and benefit several different departments. Aside from the obvious purpose of systematically relating unique numbers to unique components, each component category (and each component listing) was supplemented with any related technical, design and engineering information. Under this system, people who selected a component were provided (in a single reference source) an effective technical manual of component descriptions and performance. The structure of the numbering system was also carefully organized to assist the stockroom in arranging all of the components and materials in convenient locations. The design of each data sheet in the manual, which covered an array of similar components (such as machine screws) specified the varieties of such components that were commonly stocked in-house, and which varieties would require approval of the project engineer before they could be selected.

It was around this time that I came to finally understand why Nolan initially asked whether I was a spy for Bally. While I was busy cataloguing and creating the new Purchased Parts Manual, I was hoping (in the back of my mind) to get a chance at building a new generation of slot machines (possibly under the Atari name). While working at Atari, I'd gained significant exposure to integrated circuit technology, and I thought it might be the perfect time (and the perfect environment) to create a new machine.

When I mentioned this possibility, first to Al and then to Nolan, Nolan came back with an entirely different suggestion. "What can you suggest if we wanted to go into the pinball business?" I could see that he was quite serious, and told him that I would research and write up a report. It took me about six weeks to finish the research and prepare the analysis. The report began with what seemed a pertinent suggestion, "Bally, Gottlieb and others each had 50 plus years of pinball-building experience, and the world really didn't need 'just another pinball product line,' unless something unique was introduced. However, if Atari could solve four major problems, in regards to design elements that were critical to the success of any new entry into that field, the company might become a viable competitor."

My past experiences had informed me about the existing technologies, such as the rotational-molding method for large form plastic enclosure fabrication. The fact was that I understood the challenges that Atari would face if they attempted to gain a foothold in the pinball industry. The four factors that I outlined for Atari's success included the following:

1. Cabinet Fabrication Technique:

The old-line companies had enjoyed decades of cabinet building experience, and had long held well-established fabrication shops and effective product structured tooling. However, the background in cabinet building was based on wood fabrication, a technology that originated at a time when cabinet-making labor was cheap. The expense of wood fabrication was now cost prohibitive even to the old-line companies. I proposed that Atari should produce plastic cabinets using a process called rotational molding. This molding technology had been around for decades, and was already used to produce large water tanks, as well as tubs, kayaks and even the hulls of small sailboats (including molded-in metal fittings). This kind of tooling was extremely durable and very cost effective. Considering the size and intended application of a pinball machine, rotational molding seemed the perfect, low-cost answer to Atari's pinball cabinet problem.

2. Wiring Fabrication:

Another major cost factor in the manufacturing of pinball machines was the harnessing and installation of literally miles of internal wiring throughout the enclosure that needed to be bundled using a complex and labor-intensive "tree-and-branches" installation. This technology had also evolved over the years, so I proposed that Atari consider using a more modern and less labor-intensive approach. One effective solution for installing so complex a wiring system would be the use of large format printed circuit technology. This approach, I argued in my report, would not only yield accurately repeatable wiring and vastly reduced labor costs, but would virtually eliminate the costly process of testing and trouble shooting, which had always been an inherent part of hand-wired harnessing.

3. Mechanical Actuator Mechanisms:

The single most compelling feature of a pinball machine is the action of play. Among the costliest of all of the elements of pinball construction are the electro mechanical devices that propel the ball into its pattern of random, sprightly and erratic travels. The components that motivate this action are the solenoid-actuated flippers and thumper bumpers. These parts are essentially fabrications of sheet metal and coils of wire. Among the existing manufacturers, the tooling to make these parts had been complete, and paid for, for generations. Any prospective company breaking into the field would essentially have to start over from scratch and design, tool, fabricate and inventory these items – a very costly move today. I recommended that one possible way to minimize this costly aspect would be to create a universal family of actuator subcomponents. This meant developing a basic set of two or three common coil designs, with interchangeable dimensions and carefully structured operating characteristics. The designer would also need to develop basic sheet metal components that were universally configured for use in a range of different mechanical actuators. This method would minimize the variety and cost of basic tooling, as well as the range of components that would need to be kept in constant inventory.

4. Non-Volatile Game Memory:

One inherent advantage to electric pinball circuitry was the electromechanical nature of the system. In this system, the displayed number counters and stepping switch mechanisms automatically hold their status during any form of power outage. It was easy for a designer to create a game that will simply hold the status of any game in progress, even during a power outage. Such a machine would be set to just continue the game when the power returns – even holding any score that the player had previously attained.

Electronic logic however, is inherently volatile meaning that the status of an electronic logic circuit would not be retained during an outage. Any "game in progress" would be lost during an outage. The key to success is for the designer of any electronic pinball machine to provide a means to retain all aspects of the game in progress.

Mechanical number (score) displays, for example, could still be used to handle the problem. The remaining problem of volatile electronic logic must still be meaningfully handled in the design of an Atari product using a logic base.

I organized my concerns and recommendations in my report to Nolan on the assumption that the ideas would be recognized – not as reasons not to go into the business – but as cautionary notes and potential solutions when problems arose during the venture. It was hoped that additional research into the issues I'd raised would be conducted, but nothing seemed to materialize on the subject of pinball machines for almost another two years.

When I finally sensed that interest in the project had reignited, it appeared as though discussions had already been in the works for some time. I found it curious that after the efforts I'd put out that no one would have informed me of the direction that Atari was taking. In fact, it was only through a casual conversation with a fellow Atari employee that I happened to find out what had apparently been in the works for at least three months.

When I approached Al about the matter, he told me that the company was so concerned about the cost of starting a new venture that they had needed to engage people with substantial experience in pinball design. In fact, they'd already hired two engineers who had previously worked for Gottlieb (one of the biggest of the old-line pinball companies) each with more than 10 years of experience. I don't recall if it was Al that I asked or someone else who was closely involved in the new Pinball Division, but I questioned whether these new engineers had read my report.

Sadly they informed me that when one of the engineers received the binder, he simply wheeled around, without even cracking the cover, and dropped it into the wastebasket, saying, "I don't need anyone to tell me how to design a pinball machine!" That response gave me a vague sense of impending disaster, and a sense of foreboding in regards to the future of this project.

The situation reminded me of a story about famed architect Frank Lloyd Wright. He was a man who was well known for his flamboyant nature and as a result, was constantly being followed by reporters. On one particular occasion, he'd been called upon to give evidence in a civil case, and when he was asked to identify himself by the court clerk, his response was, "I am Frank Lloyd Wright, the world's greatest living architect." When leaving the court, he was stopped by one of the reporters and asked why he'd said that.

His reply was characteristic, "I had to." he said. "I was under oath." This tale reinforced my view that arrogance was not a particularly desirable trait, even for those who are entitled to it.

About a year later, Atari executives asked me to be a part of a new design team to troubleshoot some technical difficulties with one of the new pinball products. This was my first chance to really discover what was going on in the division, and to actually see the machines that were already built and being marketed. What I discovered was quite astonishing, particularly considering the people who had been the driving force behind this product. It was at this point that I'd heard that Atari had already invested $1 million into this project and was desperately trying to recoup its investment.

My first sight of their new creation was both amazing and shocking. First, the game play was truly amazing! I had never seen a play field as complex, active, or dramatic as the one they conceived and turned into reality. There were at least two levels of playing fields above the main board surface, giving the ball action a substantial vertical component. Massively articulated lighting had been skillfully combined with sound that was unlike anything I'd ever heard. All of this sparkle and spectacle combined to yield a game with vastly expanded player interest and player participation.

Management was really getting concerned with the marketing problems surrounding the game. All of the new player-interest bells and whistles were unable to mask the basic equipment design flaws – flaws that unfortunately drew the negative attention of the arcade owners. Who after all, were the people who were expected to buy these games (not the players)?

For a start, the game cost twice the amount of any other pinball machine on the market. Worse yet, the overall machine was one and a half times the width of any other game, which was a huge deterrent in terms of critical arcade floor space. There was no doubt that the machine would see substantially more play than more conventional games. The question of whether or not this product could actually draw enough more in revenue, to offset its purchase price, severely limited the marketability. In addition, there was the very real earnings concern on the part of the potential buyer, when he realized that three players, playing three different machines, would earn 50%

more, in the same amount of time, than two players playing two machines, in the same floor space. This reality only served to compound the problem, that the Atari machine would take twice as long to recover the purchase price, as compared with any conventional product. In my opinion, the mistake of designing a game under a philosophy that was centered around player appeal, rather than the fundamental needs of the arcade owners, inevitably lead to the failure of Atari's pinball marketing dreams.

The marketing problems, from my point of view, were only part of Atari's faulted Pinball product strategy. For instance, none of my voiced concerns in regards to manufacturing cost had apparently been given the slightest consideration. For example, no effort was made to determine the practicality of rotational molding for cabinets, and the expense of the conventional wooden cabinets must have been a major product cost factor. Neither had anyone properly addressed the issue of wire harnessing, again as a cost driver. The strangest decision, it seemed to me, was the determination to buy electro-mechanical actuator elements (e.g., flippers, thumper-bumpers, etc.), from Gottlieb or from Bally at outrageous prices! This one decision alone placed Atari under the constant threat of having critical components suddenly (and possibly strategically) made unavailable by their most serious market competitors!

To a minor degree, this entire episode reminded me of my experiences at TJM, and the possible involvement of Bally in that former company's ongoing disasters. For instance, could there possibly have been some linkage between the noted (seemingly plausible) design flaws, coupled to the erroneous marketing philosophy (designing to players rather than to buyers), with the fact that former Gottlieb people were engineering Atari's products? Not withstanding these misty concerns, I never expressed my suspicions, either to Al or to Nolan. Nonetheless, it remains a nagging possibility that this entire episode was in fact an example of a perfect, self-cleaning scam, worked upon Atari by some very clever competitors.

From 1973 to 1975, Atari remained a whirlwind of activity, and the perfect place to work for anyone with a creative spirit and the skills to turn a whimsical idea into working hardware. Any single idea could become the next Pong, no matter who might have thought of it.

Pong had been Nolan's first and greatest success for the company, and since its debut, the coin-operated video game market had absorbed tens of thousands of these machines. The game was so popular that it was expanded into new markets overseas, such as Japan and various countries in Europe. To feed what seemed an unquenchable consumer demand, elaborate equipment was brought into the plant to automatically load IC (Integrated Circuit) chips and other related components onto an endless run of game circuit boards. Then, as with any fashionable product, the time came when the insatiable public seemed to be satisfied. They were beginning to want more. The attention span of the consumer as well as the arcade operators was getting shorter, and they sought out games with more variety – games that were faster, newer and more diverse. Public demand for Pong started to slow significantly, backlogging the factory storeroom in the U.S. and the overseas warehouses with thousands of unsold circuit boards. Management took the option of selling off the overseas operations and inventories at wholesale to recover working capital. Nolan was not one to give up the game just because of slow sales. After some heavy brainstorming sessions, the staff came up with two solutions. One solution was to create a new line of street video games. To fill the gap until the new products could be created, they would find new markets for basic Pong, but using different applications. These new versions of the game would absorb the huge overrun of circuit boards that had flooded the stock room before the production line slowed and eventually shut down. Atari swiftly targeted all sorts of possible applications. Game boards were installed into cabinets that looked like small bedside tables, with 12-inch monitors that were mounted with their screens facing upward. No coin play was needed, since these machines were planned for waiting rooms of doctors, dentists or other professional offices. These games were simply intended to entertain clients waiting for service. Similar games, but with coin operation were built literally into salvaged barrels, coffee table style, to yield the kind of character suited to bars and lounges. Atari even packaged coin-operated games for installation directly into glass-covered bar tops.

While on the surface these methods seemed like a sure fire way to generate desperately needed income, the strategies were saddled with serious problems. The plans proved to be a heavy drain on product development resources, without quite yielding the level of income needed to survive. The actual extent of the shortfall became evident to me when I was developing a cabinet design and needed some custom hardware.

When I contacted one of our usual suppliers to acquire these specialized components, I was told that material sales to Atari were on hold pending payment of overdue statements.

Then, like the last minute thunder of the in-riding cavalry, the creative genius of the Grass Valley R&D crew began to pour their new game products into our design offices. War games were becoming increasingly popular, and designs for machines like Tank, Anti-Aircraft and Battleship were now jumping off our desks. Other products, like Quack, where the player (as a duck-hunter) fired light-beam rifles at the video screen, soon followed. The real winner was a game called Gran-Trak, which allowed someone to drive a car-like symbol around a meandering racetrack trying to beat the clock. A few obstacles were also thrown in, such as invisible skid-prone oil slicks, and a crash would cost the player points. The romping success of this game led immediately to the building of Gran-Trak II, a two-driver game, which added the element of competition to the mix. Sales rocketed, leading to the creation of a four-driver version. That machine was packaged like a large table, with players positioned around each side with the video screen pointed upwards in the center. The cars were displayed using different colors so that each player would recognize their car. Gran-Trak grew in popularity, and soon the product line was enlarged to its ultimate complexity of eight players. At this point, the game design hit a minor snag.

One of the engineers walked into my office after he'd finally completed the initial prototype of the eight-racer machine. He was carrying the harness-terminated power supply board (the circuit that converts the 110 wall outlet power into five-volts DC). That was the voltage needed to energize all of the IC logics.

He held it out to me, gripping the harness like a dead rat, and asked me, "What the hell happened?"

The nature of the problem was obvious to me, but what was more surprising was the fact that it wasn't obvious to him. Only over time did I learn that many of these game logic engineers could do amazing, magical tricks with the microchips that were seemingly like tinker toys and chess pieces in their possession. Power supplies and power circuitry seemed to remain a complete mystery to them. The fact was that all of the main current-carrying circuit traces had been fried – literally blown off the circuit board! The circuit design of this power supply, and the circuit board that carried the wiring, had initially been developed for the first Gran-Trak game. Moreover, it would function equally as well when it was installed (without change) into Gran-Trak II (even though a second driver circuit was added). The second driver circuit meant that twice the supply current would be drawn. When the designers later created the four-player game, they naturally installed more hefty power supply components, but mounted them onto the same basic printed wiring board. Four of the driver-game boards were then employed, needing four times the current. When the designers tried the same trick to power the eight driver-game using the same printed wiring board, the traces on the power supply circuit board couldn't handle yet another doubling of the current power level. The wiring traces were then so trivial that they simply behaved like fuses – poof! I was astonished that these genius-grade IC circuit engineers weren't able to figure out a simple power equation that would've told them that they needed to "heavy up" the circuit traces on the power supply board. Within 24 hours, I'd created a new circuit board artwork with proper-sized traces, and the new boards were ordered before the end of the week.

My work at Atari seemed to bring new challenges daily, but rather than being overwhelmed by them, they actually served as reminders of what made my job worth doing. Above all, the Atari experience was my first real introduction into the design and practical application of integrated circuits – with hands-on experience in TTL logic (transistor-transistor logic). It was a long, slow process of assisted self-education, but before I left the company, I had cultivated my skills in TTL logic so I could do serious logic circuit design, in a format known as conditional-logic.

Moreover, whether it was my gift of gab, or interpersonal skills, management saw fit to casually "promote" me to the title of international field service engineer. In this role, I was obliged to meet and entertain visiting representatives from Atari's overseas customers, such as Atari-Japan. This position was yet another learning experience for me, and one that gave me my first really close contact with other cultures from around the world. The meet-and-greets and dining engagements with overseas representatives engaged me in fascinating conversations, and provided wonderful insight and appreciation into the lives and traditions of other cultures.

My first meeting with the representatives of Atari-Japan was an interesting example. The local steak house in Los Gatos (where Atari was then located) was exceptionally good at hosting luncheons – or so we thought. As quality conscious as that restaurant had been, this time they really loused it up. One of my guests had ordered steak. Soon after it was placed before him, I noticed that he was having more than a little trouble chewing it. In fact it looked as if that serving had come from between the steer's horns! I saw him at his third attempt at chewing a bite, when I was finally obliged to call the waiter over to complain, and insist that they try again – and this time serve something edible. The server was most accommodating, and immediately took the plate from beneath the man's knife and fork. My guest exhibited astonishment that verged upon shock that the waiting staff would actually serve him another steak – without an added charge. Later when I recounted the affair to Nolan, he explained to me why the Japanese gentleman was so amazed at the service. In Japan, there is almost no homegrown beef, and what beef there is, is usually beer-fed and (believe it or not) hand massaged! Limited amounts of beef are imported, usually from Australia. As a result, steak in Japan is a rare delicacy, and even in the mid-1970s commonly cost a minimum of $100 per serving!

I recall another particularly intriguing conversation that I had with a gentleman from Brazil who, during the course of our conversation, described a major construction project in progress in his country. In an effort to expand "civilization" into their vast and previously undeveloped interior, Brazil had built a remarkable new city, virtually in the middle of the jungle called Brazilia. For months, crews were constructing a highway that would join the new city with the coast – a construction that was literally hacking its way through a forest of green hell. As my guest was describing the perils of the venture, he commented that one of the difficulties the workers faced was that it was illegal to kill an Indian.

He immediately noticed my reaction to his statement that the workers should regard this restriction as a difficulty, and instantly expanded his explanation with the comment, "I mean that it's illegal to kill an Indian – even if he's trying to kill you!"

These experiences were only small examples of such revelations gained from encounters with clients and other guests from Thailand, Central America, South Africa, France, Italy, England, and Germany.

In addition to hosting dozens of foreign reps, Nolan soon began inviting me to attend other business luncheons, not only with overseas clients, but also with top executives from our U.S. customer base. At first, to be perfectly honest, I really felt like a fish out of water. Marketing was never really my forte. I was in constant fear that at some point I would really put my foot in my mouth! Sure enough, on one particular occasion, a waiter was taking drink orders from the guests. Since I didn't drink, I simply ordered a ginger ale. Just then I caught sight of Nolan looking daggers at me from across the table. Later he pulled me aside to say that at any future business luncheon with clients, I should at least order a highball, even if I didn't drink it. This question of protocol sort of bothered me. I had no idea of how to properly deal with it, until I asked a friend what I should do.

He countered by asking if I liked soda pop. I said, "Sure." Then he said, "Your problem is solved. Next time, just order a Sloe-Gin Fizz. You'll love it!"

So at the next luncheon, I did exactly that and immediately caught a glimpse of Nolan's approving smile. I tried the cocktail and found it quite tasty – so much so that when the waiter returned, I ordered another one. I think it was after the third drink that my transmission locked. At the conclusion of the meal, I congratulated myself on aiming for the middle of the three doors that my corrupted vision presented me. After this episode, I came to understand the meaning of moderation, in the acceptance of good advice.

My introduction to business etiquette was well timed. Nolan soon informed me that he would accompany me during the first few weeks of a three-month stint to Europe to meet with prospective distributors of Atari equipment. After those first few weeks, I was essentially left alone with the decision-making power to determine whether or not certain prospective distributors had facilities that were properly staffed and equipped to adequately repair and maintain the game circuit boards of Atari's equipment. If so, they would be qualified as exclusive Atari distributors for that particular area.

Years earlier, when Atari's only product had been Pong, it was the company's practice to ship the complete game, cabinet and all. By the time I'd entered on the scene, Atari was sending only the internal circuit boards, wiring harnesses, and any essential panel controls that were peculiar to a particular game product. Marketers (or equipment buyers) were then left to supply their own cabinets and video monitors.

I'd heard one interesting story, from an Atari employee who'd been an overseas tech, and was present when the first crated game was opened at a marketer's shop in London. This particular machine had been sent with exactly the same cabinet and graphics that were used at the time in the United States, with the exception that the circuit power supply that had been modified to operate on 250 volt, 50 Hz. AC (The outlet power provided throughout England). The tale went on to describe the English technical team's astonishment when they pulled off the cover of the box for their first sight of the circus-colored game and saw the bold, graphic lettering "P-O-N-G" emblazoned across the front panel. You can understand how things get lost in translation when you understand that "Pong" is a British colloquialism for passing wind. In essence, Atari had shipped them a game that was boldly headlined (in their view), "F-A-R-T." Such are the curious subtleties and hazards of international business.

So now it was my turn to charm the British and the continental Europeans, and to confirm that these marketers were ready to handle Atari's distribution needs. My trip started calmly enough with a flight to New York and then a change of planes for the trans-Atlantic flight to Madrid. There was a problem at LaGuardia with the previously scheduled plane and crew, so our flight into Barajas (Bah-ra-has) Airport in Madrid arrived two hours behind schedule. Dawn was just breaking as our flight landed and taxied to a stop in the middle of the tarmac, well away from the terminal.

I yawned, stretched and glanced out the window, and immediately asked the person next to me, "What year is this?"

It was 1975, of course, and Spain was still under the rule of General Francisco Franco. Only moments after stopping, men in World War II-era Nazi uniforms surrounded the plane! During the mid-1930s, Franco's military had been equipped by Germany's Nazi government. Leading the airport military contingent was a woman dressed in a dark khaki jacket and riding breaches, a red beret, dark sunglasses, carrying a riding crop, and (of course) wearing a pistol belt. The soldiers, who'd encircled the plane, were armed with rifles and were standing "at the ready," as the lady-lead officer came aboard to escort all of us out onto a large bus – with no seats.

The first thought that ran through my head was, "I guess "Wayne" is alright, but I wonder if they knew that my father's name was Vinitski?"

All of the passengers quietly shuffled off the plane to the waiting bus. As the bus drove across the tarmac, I noticed that the buildings surrounding the airfield still appeared to have bullet holes from the days of the Spanish Civil War – no joke! My apprehensions were soon abated as the bus delivered us, undisturbed, to the customs facilities in the main terminal building. I later learned that the reason for the military presence, including the fellows who were wandering the terminal with Thompson sub-machine guns, were part of a security team that had been mobilizing against a terror threat from Basque separatists.

Finally reunited with my luggage, I hailed a cab and began my journey. Atari had arranged for me to stay at the Eurobuilding Hotel, then the only five-star hotel in Madrid. After freshening up a bit, I was greeted downstairs by a driver from Segasa, a company that marketed and operated coin entertainment equipment throughout Madrid and the surrounding areas. Segasa was the first company on my list to be evaluated. Moreover, this was my first experience with a technical facility located in a country that was technologically a full generation behind the United States, and much of the world as well. I learned that the Franco government, for example, had placed heavy restrictions on the importation of electronic components and equipment. In fact, it was my understanding that there were only a dozen or so integrated circuit engineers in all of Spain, and curiously enough, four of them worked for Segasa.

As I was touring Segasa's maintenance facilities, I noticed that the technicians were testing integrated circuit boards, using common pointer-type voltmeters. The problem with this practice was that IC circuits operate on precisely 5-volts, plus/minus 5% – and the pointer-type meters that the techs were using, also have only an inherent accuracy of plus or minus 5%. This meant that the accuracy of their meters was not precise enough to honestly tell them whether or not the circuit under test was exhibiting the proper operating voltage.

I asked the lead technician if they had any digital (electronic) voltmeters in the shop and he responded with, "Digital what?" To clarify my question, I took a hand-held digital meter out of my traveling case to help explain.

Suddenly, I was surrounded by lab techs essentially asking, "Where's your spaceship parked?" It was then that I realized that there was no chance for me to get out of that building alive without relinquishing that meter. It took about an hour for me to get hold of Nolan back in California who immediately gave me permission to leave my tester behind. Segasa, of course, passed its qualification with flying colors.

A few days later, I was on a plane again, this time landing at the Charles de Gaulle Airport in Paris, where I was greeted by Monsieur Guillard of Socademics. He was the youthful son of the company's owner. Socademics was then the central distribution facility for Atari's equipment throughout Europe. Young Monsieur Guillard was a master linguist and served as a huge asset to me. It was a great relief to have his company and assistance, since my mastery of French was extremely limited. In fact, I knew about six good words in that language, only four that could safely be used in public. My Italian was even worse, and that country was next on my immediate schedule. Young Guillard turned out to be the perfect host for the next three months of my journey, not only providing exceptional verbal liaison throughout my travels in France and Italy, but was also diligent in providing me with delightful local experiences and entertainments during my leisure time.

As an American in a foreign country, and as a representative of Atari, I wanted to respect the culture, but to be candid; when it came to food I was (and remain) predominantly a "meat-and-potatoes" man. However, there is one category of food that I have difficulty tolerating and that's fish! Nonetheless, I told myself that since I was a corporate agent, no matter what my hosts would serve me, I would eat it – period. What I hadn't yet realized was that my determination would be tested on my first evening in Paris.

Monsieur Guillard, no doubt playing the most gracious host, thought it would be a treat to take me to the oldest seafood restaurant in the city. I gritted my teeth and smiled with gracious acquiescence, thinking to myself, "I can do this! I know I can. It's just a matter of self control."

The opulence of the restaurant was something out of a movie set. The entire menu, of course, was in French and since I couldn't read a word of it, I allowed my host to order for me. During the next two hours, an uncountable number of courses were placed before me. To this day I have no idea what those foods were (and I probably didn't want to know), but I freely admit that everything at that dinner table was delicious! I'd survived my first great test.

Most of my experiences under Guillard's guidance were absolutely delightful – except for one occasion that I found to be truly strange. On one particular evening, Guillard took me to a formal dinner party at the home of a family friend who was a German national. It was an occasion, I suppose, he thought I'd enjoy. Our host was quite a successful businessman who'd amassed a fortune by leasing cargo ships worldwide, but he was also a man with political views that were greatly at odds with anything of my experience. Moreover, I noticed the other French guests at the table, (curiously enough) appeared to hold attitudes in sympathy with his. I found this quite unusual, considering my presumption of what a Frenchman's thinking would most likely have been regarding World War II. During the course of the conversation (a conversation that surprisingly was conducted almost entirely in English), there was an increasingly unnerving atmosphere, where I found myself to be psychologically "out of tune."

Looming large in my thoughts was the old adage, "Better to remain silent, and be thought a fool than to open your mouth and remove all doubt." Or perhaps it was more like, "Discretion is the better part of valor."

As we approached dessert, the political tone of the conversation became unmistakable, when our host commented, "The only reason that Germany lost the war is because the United States came in on the wrong side. What do you think, Herr Wayne?"

It had been surprising enough to witness such pro-German sentiments throughout the dinner, especially among the company of Frenchmen, but I was totally unprepared for a question to be directed towards me. It caught me completely off guard. I quickly recalled the definition of a diplomat as "someone who could tell you to go to hell, in a way that makes you look forward to the trip." In light of this, I made the most diplomatic reply I could think of. "At the outbreak of World War II," I said, "The American public was not psychologically attuned to Hitler and the Nazi philosophy." A good-natured chuckle drifted around the table, and the conversation shifted at once to another topic. It seemed my first test in diplomacy had been a success!

My trips across Europe continued. Over the next several weeks, Guillard and I traveled by way of the Orient Express to Dijon and then on to Besancon in France, near the Swiss border. Afterwards, by way of Air France, we spent several days in Turin, Italy, where I met and qualified the main Italian distributor, Monsieur Bertolino. In order to celebrate the occasion, our host immediately took us off to yet another upscale restaurant. (All in all, I think I gained ten pounds on that European tour.) It was at this particular luncheon, however, that yet another colorful conversation unfolded. By the time of this tour Atari had expanded into a broad range of military-type games, such as Battleship, Submarine Force, Tank and Anti-Aircraft. Since Socademics was Atari's central distribution source, our newly qualified host was anxious to express to Guillard the variety and quantities of games he would immediately need and forcefully expressed those demands.

"Monsieur Guillard," he began, "my needs at the moment are at least six battleships, twelve tanks, two submarines and ten anti-aircraft!"

As diplomatically as possible, Guillard replied, "That's impossible! At least half of what you're asking for has been committed to London, and five of the tanks you want are already being shipped to Belgrade."

It was during this banter between Guillard and Bertolino that I glanced around the room, noticing the number of heads that were uncomfortably turning in our direction. Finally, I had to kick Guillard in the ankles to get him to see that the drift of his conversation could possibly get us all arrested! With a sheepish grin, his understanding was quickly conveyed to Bertolino, and the subject shifted at once to female conquests.

After Turin, we headed back to Paris for some leisure time. A day or two later, my host won my undying gratitude by introducing me to the world's oldest flea market, which had stood on the same site for the past 300 years. This market was unlike anything I'd ever experienced. It covered many acres, sported every kind of trading outlet from elaborate and well-stocked stores to a fellow who stood on a street corner, dealing trinkets out of a cap. Among the various objects that this particular dealer had to offer were three French silver coins from their Third Republic.

On my request, young Guillard asked how much the dealer wanted, and the answer came back, "Fifty francs." At an equivalent of over $12, I thought that was a bit too much, and asked my friend to offer him forty.

A rather animated conversation (in French) then passed back and forth between the men, until final Guillard said, "He's adamant. He wants fifty."

Then as I dropping the coins back into the fellow's hat, we turned to walk away – when in a clear, crisp English voice he called after us, "Forty-five!"

I bought the coins.

Through the guidance and tutelage of Guillard over several weeks, I was able to pick up enough of the French language to comfortably make my way around Paris on my own. I decided to start with a tour of the Eiffel Tower, just about five blocks from my hotel. At the tower, I was offered the choice of the stairs, or for a few more francs, I could opt for the elevator. Being a budget conscious sort of guy, I opted for the stairs.

That evening, in one of my few letters home to mama about my trip, I wrote, "When one forgets that he's 40 years old, there's nothing like a walk up the Eiffel Tower to remind him!"

The next day, I was determined to enjoy a less demanding experience around the city, and decided on a self-guided tour of the Louvre. My immediate goal was to experience a viewing of the Mona Lisa. As I gazed upon the portrait, I quickly came to realize why this painting is considered to be among the greatest artworks of all time. I can also advise that no photo image can ever convey its astonishing qualities that are only perceived through a first-hand observation. Leonard da Vinci's technique of adding colors, layer upon layer for nearly 10 years, yields a visible, glass-like depth that's impossible to reproduce. There was another aspect to my viewing that I found totally fascinating. The picture was housed in a large, square, wood-paneled room with Parquet flooring – a room where 15 other historic artworks were also on display. The Mona Lisa was set inside a glass-covered niche with a well-aged guard seated next to it. The guard, it seemed to me, was at least the same age as the painting (though no cobwebs were evident). There were some 20 people or so viewing the painting at the same time and they formed a half-circle around the glass. At the same time, only about 10 feet away hung two other astonishing examples of da Vinci's work: The Virgin of the Rocks and John the Baptist. It was interesting to note that the Mona Lisa viewers all but ignored these two paintings, which in my opinion were equal in quality and grandeur to the Mona Lisa.

During my tour, I never realized how vast the Louvre really was, and unfortunately, since I'd arrived late in the morning, I was obliged to spend my few hours literally running though the massive building, and was still only able to view a tenth of the exhibits. One display that truly impressed me was a fully restored common room of Louis XIV, complete with the room's original furnishings. As I'd described earlier in this book, among my fondest childhood memories were my visits to the Cleveland Art Museum, and its remarkable section on Egyptology. You can appreciate my astonishment when I realized that the entire Cleveland Art Museum could have been lost within the Louvre's Egyptology Department! In hindsight, I should have realized that the Louvre's Egyptian exhibits would surely be exceptional, given the amount of time that Napoleon's armies had spent there, and the hundreds of tons of Egyptian artifacts Napoleon and his forces brought back to France. My advice to anyone who might visit the Louvre in the future is to allow at least three full days, if not a full week, to fully appreciate not only the Egyptian experience, but also all of the amazing treasures within that marvelous museum.

As I continued my tour of Paris, I took an opportunity to wonder at many of the other great monuments in the city, including the Luxor Obelisk (so often ignored by most tourists). It was originally one of a pair of Obelisks that had been constructed over 3,000 years ago, and had stood for nearly all that time at the Temple of Luxor in Egypt before it was brought to Paris. This artifact, hewn from a single block of red granite, towers over 70 feet in height and weighs in excess of 200 tons (nearly four million pounds). The Luxor Obelisk had originally been a gift to Louis X by the Egyptian viceroy, Mehemet Ali. Then in 1836, French King Louis Phillip ordered his engineers to set the object up in the Place de la Concorde, as a gift to the people of France, supposedly as an atonement or forgiveness for the hellish tragedies experienced so many decades ago,

Besides the magnificence of the object itself, it is an astonishing achievement to have been able to dismount a massive, singular piece of a solid object from its original resting place, and then transport it down the Nile and across the Mediterranean, especially given the technological limitations of the time. The final stage of this miraculous effort was the monument's continuing journey to Paris and the Herculean task of its faultless erection on site. Not only did this ancient Egyptian artifact survive the travel, but it also endured the hellish threats of the Franco-Prussian War and two subsequent world wars. Yet it still lives on in the age of the modern world for visitors to wonder upon.

I was determined not to appear foolish or uninformed on the history and treasures of Europe to my hosts. I almost succeeded. One day, as I was being driven through Paris, I commented to Guillard, "The architecture is really amazing, like that building, styled in Louis XIV." My host replied with a tone of determined diplomacy.

"No, it is not styled in Louis XIV – It *is* Louis XIV." At that moment, I think I may have visibly shrunk at least six inches.

I met my ultimate test in determined diplomacy on my final evening in Paris. As a proper farewell, my young host chose to honor me by taking us to his favorite eatery, L'Escargot. That did it! I summoned all of my courage and as diplomatically as possible, I commented to my host, "This place is truly magnificent, but please tell me that there's something on this menu that isn't made with snails?"

With a grin, Guillard replied, "Not to worry. We have a real treat for you." Within half an hour the waiter placed before me, the most magnificent filet mignons I had ever tasted. It cut like butter, and if there were any snails around it, they were damned well hidden.

Next stop on my itinerary: London. After weeks in an environment where the common language was either French or Italian, I finally found myself among folks whose language I could understand – well, just about. My first language barrier happened shortly after being ensconced at the Dorchester Hotel. It was a brilliant bit of architecture, right out of the 1920s. It was four stories high, beautifully appointed, but in any sort of a breeze, the whole building shook. The rooms were very comfortable and the food was quite good.

However, even before leaving the States, I had been dealing with an aggressive case of athlete's foot on two of my toes. I had packed a sufficient stock of medication, but an insufficient supply of Bandaids, which I was now desperate to replenish.

I rushed from the hotel, and hailed a taxi, instructing the driver, "Take me to a drug store, fast as you can."

The driver turned around, with a quizzical, shifty-eyed expression, and said in a stern, but subdued tone, "Not here, mate! Not here!" In an instant I realized my mistake.

"Sorry! I mean I need to get to a 'chemist' as soon as possible!" To this day, I've had the distinct impression that the fellow was truly disappointed – as if he thought he really had a "live one." Then when I finally got to the chemist, it took me another 10 minutes to realize that Band-Aids in England were called "plasters." There I was – once again in the language learning business.

Language barrier aside, I also had problems convincing the British that there were noteworthy places to visit in the United States. One of our clients was considering a trip to the States, and asked about sights of interest, particularly along the Atlantic coast. I suggested that he might find Williamsburg, Virginia, an interesting place to visit. I noted there was a fully restored Colonial Village that had been founded in 1607.

He replied, "Really? The tavern, down the street from my house, sports a fireplace that dates back to the time of William the Conqueror in the 11th century!"

Aside from these cultural differences, my time in England was instructive, often exciting, and quite pleasurable – except that this was the only country during my trip where I suffered a bout of food poisoning. On one particular occasion, my English host and I were obliged to drive from London, north to the town of Chester, very near to the sight of Hadrian's Wall (from Roman times). I had overslept and missed breakfast before my host arrived with the car. We were halfway to our destination when I noted a diner built directly over the motorway, so that motorists headed in either direction could access it. Quite a clever arrangement, I thought. I told my associate that I was getting quite hungry and asked if we could stop. His reluctance seemed strange to me at the time, but I ignored it. It was stranger still, when we walked up into the nearly empty eatery, and he simply looked on while I helped myself to a variety of foods set up buffet-style. There were scrambled eggs, bacon, orange juice, toast and some coffee, and it all looked very tasty. When we finally sat down at a table it became clear why my companion wasn't joining me at a seemingly pleasant breakfast. Not a single item I'd selected, including the coffee, proved palatable. In short, if you want good food during your European travels, go to Italy or France.

On this excursion, I also became conscious of another curious fact. In England, the plumbing was all of the latest manufacture, but far too often it didn't seem to work very well, like the shower in my hotel room in Chester. The shower yielded only two squirting columns of water, one to the navel and the other to my left eye. On the other hand, in France, the plumbing was often a century old or more and was always flowing. At least, the stall in the English shower was small enough that there wasn't any chance of falling.

As I continued my tour of England, I found that most of the potential Atari vendors had no problem becoming certified. The best vendors were located in London and easily passed the certification process. This wasn't surprising, however, since many of them had worked closely with Atari for a number of years. The only reason I was sent to review their personnel and credentials was to make certain their technical facilities had advanced sufficiently to handle the more advanced of Atari products.

In England, as in France and Italy, I confess I spent very little time doing actual work for Atari, and more time enjoying the sights as a tourist. The British Museum, of course, was first on my list of must-sees, followed by the original Madame Tussaud's Wax Museum. I also enjoyed my first real experience at the theater, usually catching a show two or three times a week.

As the three-month stint wore on, I began to realize a few things. Among these was the fact that the work I had been sent to do was in fact so trivial that a trained monkey could have done it. In short, it finally settled into my consciousness that this whole excursion had really been nothing more than a grand perk – a sort of corporate thank you for my accomplishment of other things of real value to Atari over the preceding two years. While I truly appreciated the wonderful gesture of the trip, during my remaining years at Atari, I never let Nolan know that I'd caught on to his little secret.

When I returned to California from my European tour, I found that the Atari game-development strategy had finally become successful enough to fully support the company as an independent operation. In fact, the level of success was so high it attracted the attention of Warner Communications – so much so that they bought the entire enterprise! Unfortunately, that takeover would have a severe impact on the overall creative character of the company, and the working environment of the design and development groups. Warner, it seemed, had a different business strategy in its approach to new product development. The company's policy was not to gamble on any design or concept that didn't demonstrate a high probability for successful marketing. Executives would hold roundtable discussions to evaluate the products of Atari's competitors. Products that had already demonstrated major success on the street. In short, they willfully turned Atari away from innovation, and into a completely "me too" organization. Any kind of freewheeling, fly-by-the-seat-of-your-pants, ideas-into-hardware thinking was a thing of the past. Suddenly, it was as if the light had been extinguished in the lives of Atari designers and engineers who'd previously been conditioned to a philosophy of "What's new?" or "What's different and exciting?" Over time, the best of them moved on to other enterprises – including myself. Atari would never be the same company again.

Among the few folks who decided to stick with the new arrangement at Warner's Atari were graphics designers Pete Takaichi and Regan Cheng. As graphics designers, they were completely at home feeding their passions by continuing to create flamboyant designs for any machine. Whether the concept had originated with Atari or not, it had nothing to do with the art and imagination surrounding their collective genius. It was still an Atari design, and a Pete and/or Regan original.

One of the biggest impacts from the Warner Communications' takeover affected the Atari profit-sharing plan. From the beginning, Nolan had established a most generous mechanism where the company would share its financial gains with the people who had made the company's success possible. More than that, the system was structured to share the profits in direct proportion to each employee's actual contribution to that success. Based on a person's annual salary, a certain number of Atari shares were credited to the account of each Atarian, thereby increasing their number of shares with each year of their employment. For each year of employment, an employee also earned vested interest in their personal account of shares by an expansion of 10%. That meant if a person stayed with Atari for 10 years, they not only accumulated 10 years worth of shares, but also became fully vested in the total dollar value of that stock. Once an employee left the company, their vested interest in accumulated shares would be converted into cash, as a kind of "separation bonus." The remaining, unvested shares, if any, would then be redistributed among the "survivors" in the pool. This type of survivor's scheme was known as a "Tontine," named for its inventor, Lorenzo de Tonti, a 17th century Neapolitan banker.

However, with the takeover by Warner Communications, Nolan's profit-sharing plan came to an abrupt end. The new owners were determined to acquire every share of Atari stock, which included all of the shares in the profit-sharing accounts of every current employee. As a result, those shares each became immediately vested at the full 100%, and were then purchased at par by Warner. It was a most pleasant surprise when I received a check for $9,000 as my chunk of the immediate buyout. I used this money as the basis for my first meaningful acquisition of gold. The purchase was made at $109 per ounce.

As for Atari's founding genius, Nolan Bushnell, he decided to put his newfound gains and genius skills into his new venture – the Chuck-E Cheese line of entertainment restaurants. He founded the popular restaurant/theater chain in 1977 in San Jose, California. Unfortunately by 1984, a number of complications caused Nolan to lose control of that enterprise – an enterprise that has since passed through a range of owners and managements. Today the corporation operates over 500 entertainment centers in 48 states and several foreign countries.

PART VI
Steve Jobs – And Apple is Born

During the three and a half years that I'd worked at Atari, my job demanded a close working connection with most of the engineering staff. During this time, I'd developed a casual, but very pleasant relationship, with a young freelance engineer and game designer named Steve Jobs. Jobs was principally engaged as a consulting engineer on various Atari projects when we worked together. I found myself intrigued by his sprightly, energetic and sometimes whimsical views of the world around him. Although I was almost 20 years older than Jobs, just being around him inspired me to rethink the world and renew within myself the feeling that all things were possible. He simply resonated that kind of spirit and a related "can-do" attitude. He had a talent for sensing the value in new products and particularly new ideas. I could see that his character possessed an underlying drive to establish some kind of business enterprise of his own one day. While we engaged in our project work, Jobs and I would find time to chat about life's intriguing twists and turns, and potential enterprises and activities. It was during one of these conversations that I mentioned the history of my experiences in the jaded world of slot machines. A short time later, he mentioned that he had access to $50,000, and asked me if I would consider getting back into the slot machine development game.

My response to him was both direct and instructive, "That would be the quickest way I could think of to lose $50,000." The subject never came up again.

Over the next few months, Jobs and I would often meet for lunch, and on occasion, he'd come over to my apartment for dinner or just for conversation. The thing I found most interesting about our discussions was that there was no limit to the range of topics. For instance, he asked me whether I thought that the stock market would ever break the $1,000 mark. The market at that time had been flirting with that benchmark for quite a while in the mid-1970s, but until then had never actually crossed that threshold. Jobs knew that socio-economics had been a side interest of mine for the past two decades.

I told him, "Certainly! With the economic system structured the way it is, and a monetary system based on worthless paper, I've no doubt that it'll top a thousand. It'll top 5,000! It'll top 10,000! There's really no limit."

I don't think Jobs really believed me about the stock market's potential surge. Nor did he really believe in my projections about the price of gold, or even in my reasoning behind these projections. In fact, I don't think he properly understood the underlying concepts that I was trying explain, in spite of his aptitude for grasping new ideas and thinking "outside of the box." Years later, when Jobs started to really get into the chips, so to speak, he told me that he'd actually bought $250,000 in gold, probably at around $200 per ounce. Unfortunately, because he'd missed the proper appreciation of what I was trying to explain to him, he'd made this purchase as a purely speculative venture. That is, as a method for making more paper dollars, rather than as a technique for preserving buying power. My point had been that he should hold onto the gold as long term security, but Jobs saw the involvement as a speculative venture, so when the price went up a bit, he sold the lot for $400,000. Today, that same gold would be worth $1.5 million or more.

Another fascinating memory of our conversations was an exchange that was highly revealing of Jobs's nature. It was during the time when Jobs was taking some college courses. I was slightly amazed at his truly giddy delight in learning of the core principles of the Calculus, as he was describing this understanding as a powerful design tool. It was as if Jobs had suddenly discovered a marvelous new toy, one that was possessed of limitless possibilities. I think it was this pure radiated enthusiasm that made it so exciting to be around him.

These chats encompassed many subjects, including his relationship with a fellow engineer, Steve Wozniak, and their participation in a computer club (what would come to be known as the "Homebrew Computer Club"). Among other things, he also showed great interest in the documentation and inventory control systems that I was in the process of developing at Atari. His excitement level really flared up when he described a program he was working on that was designed to simplify and enhance the art of musical composition.

I don't believe that Jobs ever saw himself as a major participant in the evolving dynamics of Atari. At the same time, he seemed to take real delight in the development of new games. In this context, with the support of Wozniak, Jobs provided the company with a very successful product called "Breakout". In this design, they took the basic Pong circuit and rearranged it so that the player was given a single paddle that could be moved horizontally, back and forth across the bottom of the screen. At the outset of the game, several layers of "bricks" were displayed across the top of the field with each layer in a different color. When the ball came into play, the player had to make sure that the ball didn't get past his paddle in its downward flight, and then rebound it upward again towards the bricks. As each brick was hit, the ball bounced downward again. As each brick was hit, it vanished and the player's score accumulated. As the player advanced through the game, the bricks in each progressively higher row were valued at a higher score than the previous layer. What's more, the player was forced to keep up with the increasing speed of the ball, as higher levels of bricks were dispatched. If a player was skillful enough to make it past the highest level of bricks, there was yet another space above that level where the ball could bounce up and down between the upper limit of the screen and the top row of bricks, like a bonus activity. As this bonus action dispatched more and more bricks, the ball would soon find a gap where it could again speed downward, but with exceptional velocity. Now the player's skills were really put to the test. Once the ball got past the player's paddle, of course, or if he'd actually succeed in the Herculean task of wiping out all the bricks, the game was over. This game turned out to be a real winner among Atari's new products, and was later succeeded by several, more elaborate versions.

I'm sure that Jobs was involved in several other game products at Atari, but I didn't have any direct involvement with those projects. Nonetheless, beyond game design and development, his spectacular skills as a maintenance technician made him a highly respected member of the contract support team at Atari.

His talent for innovation, promotion and organization truly came to life when his relationship with Steve Wozniak led to the founding of Apple. The beginnings of Apple didn't happen overnight. In fact, it was several more months before any formal plans began to gel.

All of us were committed to other projects, but Jobs seemed to be growing restless for a totally different kind of personal adventure. One day at lunch, he told me he was planning on a trip to India. There was some sort of rare, ritualistic festival that he felt strongly moved to witness in a remote, northern part of the country. With a growing anticipation of the event, he asked my opinion about the trek. To be completely candid, the whole idea made me extremely apprehensive. Even though English was the common language of the country (as a result of a century or more of British occupation), Hindi was still the most common local tongue in the wilds of the Indian interior. I was equally certain that, even as clever as Jobs was, he probably didn't know ten words of that language. I had visions running through my head, based largely on my familiarity with Kipling of truly hair-raising perils! I had no doubt that the murderous cult of Thuggee, which had been so rampant in the early decades of British India, was no longer a threat and I'd not heard of any reports of a modern resurgence of such banditry. Even so, Jobs was planning a trek into an extremely remote territory where an uncountable number of perils could present themselves. The potential for disease and the dangers of wildlife immediately came to mind, in conjunction with conventional banditry, even without the threat of Thuggee. I didn't know if he was planning to visit Kashmir, a province that remains to this day in violent dispute for possession between India and Pakistan. There were also the very real issues of food and water especially to someone who was not accustomed to that kind of wild environment. Travel and hostelry would be troubling, even without the added difficulties of verbal communication. From the moment that Jobs would disappear into that vast Indian interior, it seemed to me that any further communication with him would be extremely chancy. Nonetheless, the thought of a non-local wandering through the interior of India in the mid-1970s was enough to make anyone a little uneasy. I could only caution him to use extreme care. In fact, I think I even invented some scary tales in an effort to discourage him from undertaking such a risky venture.

As was his nature, Jobs would not be dissuaded from living out this experience. As it turned out, his focus on this adventure was coincidently linked with Atari's need to have him provide technical assistance to an Atari-related company in Europe. That company had acquired a virtual warehouse full of Pong circuit boards, many with serious problems. At the time, I was serving as one of Atari's International Field Service Engineers, and in consequence, was overwhelmed with complaint calls about a new service technician Nolan had recently sent to execute repair and rejuvenate those boards to make them market ready. Unfortunately, that technician could only best be described as a klutz. He'd proved to be totally incompetent. After a while, Nolan was forced to fire the man, and looked frantically for someone to take over the project. It was a spark of pure genius to press Jobs into undertaking the task, promising him a fat paycheck, the best accommodations, and of course, a first-class round-trip airfare. Jobs agreed to take on the job immediately with only one unusual stipulation: He wanted to trade the return airfare for cash. He also made it clear that when he finished the work, he would be "off to unknown parts." Few people knew what that meant, but I did. He was effectively saying, "India, here I come."

Jobs headed across the Atlantic, and within a matter of days the calls from Europe changed dramatically in tone. Jobs was plowing through the work like a bulldozer, and the now-serviceable circuit boards were flying out of the warehouse in rapid-fire pace. Jobs earned the highest possible praise from the client, and within a remarkably short time, the project was successfully completed. Then, just as he'd forewarned, Jobs was nowhere to be found. I'm still not certain if anyone other than me (and his family, of course) knew exactly where he was or what he'd planned to do.

Months passed with little word from him, until suddenly one day, I got into the office and discovered that Jobs had suddenly reappeared, but he wasn't the man that we knew before the trip. Jobs had always been lean and wiry, but now, if he stood sideways, you might have to look twice; otherwise, all you heard was a voice. None of us had ever seen him look that thin before. By his own account, he thought he'd come down with every disease known to man and lived to tell about it. According to Jobs, he'd successfully accomplished everything he wanted to experience during his travels. This was the Jobs that we had all come to know and love; he was, it seemed, our version of Indiana Jones.

The man recovered from the physical strains of his travels in surprising short order – remarkable return to health after the kind of physical abuse he must have endured. During the months following his return, Jobs' involvement with fellow computer club members expanded rapidly, as did his relationship with his friend, Steve Wozniak. During this time, Wozniak developed the fundamental circuitry for a basic personal computer, which eventually led to the formation of Apple Computer.

Over a period of several weeks, Wozniak volunteered a number of offhanded comments to me about what the two men were doing. These were often casual remarks about their activities and designs, and a focused indication of what they were to do, but there was one conversation in particular that stood out in my mind. One day, Jobs asked for my advice on whether he should really commit to the very exhausting and demanding effort to build a new company based on the personal computer. He was concerned that he might miss out on the development

Ron, 1976

of other interests if he concentrated on building a personal computer company with Wozniak.

My answer to Jobs was simple and direct. "That he could more easily pursue other ventures and interests after he had money in his pocket." I told him further that he really should follow that path to corporate moneymaking, but at the same time, always keep in mind one thought, "When you've succeeded, don't forget what you wanted the money for!" Over time I've come to believe he forgot that advice.

What must be made clear is that I was never actually involved with the soon-to-be-named computer enterprise until a modest philosophical difference arose between Jobs and Wozniak. This difference of opinion led Jobs to confide in me, and seek my advice on how to resolve the issue with his friend. After reflecting on the request, I invited both men to my apartment one evening. As I recall, Jobs sat on one end of the sofa and Wozniak on the other end. I myself spent most of the time during this discussion walking about the room, pacing and talking. I've always had a tendency to think best on my feet. It was fascinating to listen to the two men as they expressed their positions, and what they saw as the future goals. It didn't take me long to understand that the actual core of the dispute was both simple and fundamental.

Jobs believed in a focused commitment to the corporate point of view, and in particular, that the basic circuit concepts of Wozniak's design were central assets to the enterprise. These basic circuits were both the strength and future of the entire business operation. Wozniak, on the other hand, seemed to have a more nebulous sense of the corporate entity concept. His whole nature, to me, was the personification of the "whimsical genius." I could see (even back then) that the two of them were effectively the perfect match to form this kind of company. They were bringing two complementary, but equal skill sets and philosophies into play at one time. They would be the perfect team if their conflicting points of view did not dissolve into unsettled conflict. In this case, Wozniak, who'd originated the basic circuit concepts, took a truly parental view of his creation. He felt that even though the circuit designs were the centerpiece of the enterprise, he still wanted to reserve the right to use the concepts in other applications as well.

I quickly recognized that my place in this discussion would be a tricky one to navigate. Most disputes can often be settled with some sort of balanced compromise, where each side gets something they wanted in the first place. In this case, however, I realized there could be no such resolution, since the issue simply came down to recognizing that Wozniak's contribution of the basic circuits would be the core property of the new company – a property that could not be "shared out." Jobs was sound in his argument and I absolutely agreed with him. I was now faced with the tricky task of making this reality clear to Wozniak, while simultaneously playing the perfect diplomat. For over an hour, I verbally tiptoed over, through and around the fact that the new company needed to entirely own the rights to these circuits. Finally, Wozniak conceded and accepted the reality of that situation. My work as a diplomat had succeeded!

Apparently Jobs had been sufficiently impressed by my diplomatic performance that before the evening was over, he encouraged the three of us to form a partnership. Jobs had concluded that an ideal arrangement would be that he and Wozniak should each hold a 45% stake in the new company, and that I should retain 10% of the voting rights. Jobs felt that

TO WHOM IT MAY CONCERN:

WHEREAS, Mr. Stephen G. Wozniak (hereinafter referred to as WOZNIAK), Mr. Steven P. Jobs (hereinafter referred to as JOBS), and Mr. Ronald G. Wayne (hereinafter referred to as WAYNE), all residents of the County of Santa Clara, State of California, have mutually agreed to the formation of a company to be specifically organized for the manufacture and marketing of computer devices, components, and related material, said company to be organized under the fictitious name of APPLE COMPUTER COMPANY (hereinafter referred to as COMPANY), then

BE IT NOTED HEREWITH, that the COMPANY has been formally established in the County of Santa Clara, State of California, in conformance with all laws, statutes, and regulations of said County and State, as of the _____1ST_____ day of _____April_____ 1976, and

BE IT FURTHER NOTED HEREWITH, that by virtue of their respective con-

Apple Computer Company contract (top)

NOW THEREFORE, it is mutually agreed and understood, that this contract contains and embodies all understandings, representations, and agreements of the parties hereto, that this agreement shall represent a potential of both risk and profit, in direct proportion to each participant's percentage of holdings, and that this contract shall be binding upon, and inure to the benefit of, each of the parties herein named, their respective heirs, assigns, executors, and successors in interest.

IN WITNESS WHEREOF, this instrument has been executed by each of the parties hereto, on this _____1ST_____ day of _____April_____ 1976.

Mr. Stephen G. Wozniak (WOZNIAK)

Mr. Steven P. Jobs (JOBS)

Mr. Ronald G. Wayne (WAYNE)

Apple Computer Company contract signatures (bottom)

in the event of any future policy disputes, he could rely on my vote as tiebreaker, and that I'd come down on the side of rationality, rather than emotion.

Through my own modest business experience, including my own founding of a corporation, I'd gained some background at writing in legalese. Jobs and Wozniak allowed me to draw up the formal contract of partnership, after the details of the contract were mutually agreed upon. Three copies of the document were produced, and each was formally signed by Jobs, Wozniak, and myself.

On April 2, 1976, the partnership was formally filed at the registry office of Santa Clara County, California, under certificate number 20443. The Apple Computer Company was born. The single astonishing fact that sticks in my memory to this day is the totally casual air that encompassed that entire experience. Without the slightest clue of what was to come, of course, it was just another ordinary event on another ordinary day.

Many people have asked me where the name "Apple" originated. In truth, I haven't a clue. Jobs presented the name to me as a fixed and final determination for the company, but whether it was his own concept, or was developed jointly between Wozniak and himself, I have no idea. Strangely enough, at the time, it never occurred to me to ask how the name came about. Simply as a guess, I would say that it possibly came from the technical term "byte." From the outset "Apple" was the name, and it would best define the product and the adventure from that day forward.

I don't recall where Wozniak was working at that time, or what he was doing for a living, but Jobs remained a freelance contractor at Atari, which left him considerable freedom of time to focus on developing the new enterprise. I was still a full-time Atari employee so my free time was next to nil. Immediately after our formal company registration was completed, Jobs approached me with several little projects. Topping the list was designing a new logo. I was thoroughly amused by Wozniak's whimsical nature as well as his joyful approach to life, so much so that it encouraged me to bathe in a similar freedom of spirit. It was an attitude that found its immediate vent in my creation of the new logo. Using a pen-and-ink design, I free-formed a gothic framework that surrounded an image of Isaac Newton under the proverbial tree, with a glowing apple in the branches above his head. Within the ribbon of framework,

I lettered out the last line of a sonnet by William Wordsworth. The line seemed totally appropriate to the new venture, "A Mind Forever Voyaging Through Strange Seas of Thought, Alone." Finally, an intricately detailed ribbon, winding with several turns, was added to the upper and lower portions of the image. On this ribbon I inscribed in large Roman letters, "APPLE COMPUTER CO." Hidden within the crosshatch pen work in the lower right corner, I added my lettered name, "R.G. Wayne." Apparently it wasn't hidden deep enough, because as soon he discovered it, Jobs insisted I remove it. I obliged without objection. To be candid, while I was extremely pleased with my creation, I also recognized that the design didn't really meet the requirements of a modern logo. It was far too complicated, too busy and too subtle to satisfy the instant impact recognition demanded in today's fast-paced marketing world. The logos of Chevrolet, GE and AT&T are typical examples of the corporate symbolization of the present day, as is the very recognizable Apple logo (including its evolved variations). Nonetheless, Jobs thought enough of my humble efforts to have a very large banner created with the design, which he displayed above his marketing stall in at least one computer products show.

With the logo design completed, other tasks included the creation of the standard warranty form, as well as the Apple 1 - Operation Manual, which contained all of the essential operating instructions along with the logic diagrams and codes. I also generated a complete schematic diagram of the original system.

During the first week of my participation in the new Apple Computer Company, everything seemed to be moving along quite nicely, until some news came to light. It was positive for the company, but at the same time, disconcerting for me. Jobs, it seemed, had successfully contracted to sell 100 units of the "Apple I" computer to a retail outlet called the Byte Shop. I was told (from another source) that the Byte Shop had a terrible reputation for not paying their bills. In order to secure the deal, Jobs had to borrow $15,000 to acquire the components and materials to fill the order. Jobs had done exactly what he was supposed to do, but in the process, he had committed the company to a substantial obligation. Since our enterprise was a company and not a corporation, it was an obligation that put me personally on the hook for $1,500 if the Byte Shop did indeed live up to its reputation. If worse came to worse, I had no idea where I'd come up with that amount of money. Remember that only a few years earlier, I'd lived through my own personal corporate failure, and spent years buying back all the stock, and paying off all my creditors.

There's no question that this previous experience may have clouded my reasoning at the time, but the circumstances surrounding the Byte Shop order, and the consequent monetary obligation, brought several realities immediately into sharp focus. It was those realities that led me to go back to the Santa Clara Registry Office on April 12, 1976 and remove my name from the Apple partnership.

I haven't enough fingers and toes to count the number of times over the years that people have asked me (in pitying tones) if I'd ever regretted my decision. I will state, here and now (but probably not for the last time) that I have never regretted my action. To begin, I had no doubt whatsoever that Apple would be a very successful venture – though no one could have anticipated the actual level of that success. At the same time however, it seemed obvious that it was going to be quite a rollercoaster ride. Remember I was 42 years old at the time – the "old man" of the group – while the two Steves were in their twenties. Jobs, in particular, was an absolute whirlwind. It was like having a tiger by the tail. It took little consideration for me to conclude that if I stayed with the enterprise, I'd probably wind up the richest man in the cemetery. What's more, I had the strong feeling that Jobs saw me as someone who could very effectively organize and run the new company's documentation system. I felt that this would eventually put me into a large back office, shuffling papers for the rest of my days. Not that such a fate would be a bad thing, but for someone who had inventive passions of his own this was hardly the vision I had in mind for my future.

Let me be perfectly clear: I am as enamored with money as anyone else, but if I'd actually committed myself to the upcoming adventure, my own sense of creativity would surely have been swamped by far brighter minds than my own, and the physical strain of riding a roman candle, I felt, would probably burn me out in short order.

*****

A short time later, an event seemed to confirm that my concerns were reasonably well founded. I heard (from what source I don't recall)

Original Apple Computer Company logo, penned by Ron, 1976

that when the product was ready for delivery, the Byte Shop was shocked to learn that each of the "computers" consisted simply of the circuit board and peripherals. None of the units (as Jobs had understood the requirement) included cabinets! I never did learn how this particular impasse was resolved.

*****

Both Jobs and Wozniak knew of my decision and the reasoning behind it, and the separation passed off very quietly, without the slightest hint of animosity. Even after the separation, Jobs approached me to design a practical enclosure for the new machines, though I can't recall whether it was for the Apple I or Apple II models. As someone who was truly passionate about product packaging and industrial design, I took the project quite seriously, and gave the problem careful thought before putting pencil to paper. Rather than implementing a vertical tower (a design common in today's products) I chose a horizontal-enclosure approach, and made the keyboard into an integral part of the design concept.

Product package design is a process that demands careful attention to every aspect of manufacture and usage. A practical design starts with a structure that is ergonomically workable (suitable to ready and convenient usage by people), as well as being tolerant and compatible with the intended environment (home, office, etc). Consideration must also be given to convenient access for system maintenance. In any home or office setting, the equipment must resist fading and/or structural degradation from direct sunlight, moderate changes in temperature, and must endure spillage of all types of common fluids. In terms of manufacture ability, product materials costs are constantly weighed against application, serviceability and ease of assembly. These are only a few factors that influence a product's development, and decisions relating to these factors inevitably affect the success or failure of the final product.

While considering these design factors for the Apple I enclosure, I reasoned that this was an initial offering of a completely new product, one that may or may not have proven successful during its first inception. This meant that I needed to come up with a design that could be inexpensively hand-assembled with a minimum of relatively low-cost components. It also implied that the components (fittings, panels, etc.) should be able to be fabricated virtually without the expense of custom tooling. By this approach, if redesign became necessary, we would avoid the need to expensively modify or even discard costly fabrication tools.

Following this line of thinking, I decided on a concept that consisted of two wooden side panels that could be conveniently profiled into a pleasing geometrical shape, and fabricated using standard production woodshop tools and simple fixtures. These panels would be spaced apart by a formed, rectangular aluminum sheet that would be shaped to cover the bottom, the back and a portion of the top of the machine, thus creating a basic box structure. To enhance the appearance, I planned for the use of plated brushed-aluminum bands to be easily assembled and installed around the edges of the panel profiles. A flat, hinged cover was added to the top of the assembled frame and would be used to support the mass of any conventional video monitor.

In addition to this highly effective, functional, and low-cost design, I added one innovative feature. It was a slideable "tambour door," similar to those commonly used on roll top desks. This door was positioned over the keyboard in such a way that when it was pulled down (to open), the articulated design would allow the door to slip in under the enclosure base. Moreover, the act of sliding the door open would turn the computer

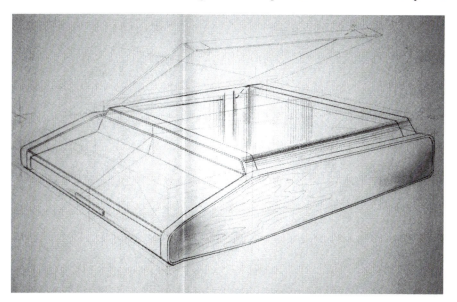

Apple I Enclosure Design

on, while sliding it upwards to close would turn the machine off. The idea behind this concept was to keep dust, cigarette ashes and other debris out of the keyboard crevices (at least while the machine was turned off.) To this date, I've never seen this idea implemented in any computer design. Then, I suppose it has only been 35 years, and it takes a bit of time for good ideas to finally come into practice.

The Apple Company never produced a prototype of my proposed design. Yet it was many months later when I learned that Jobs and Wozniak had invested $50,000 into tooling for an injection molded (or possibly foam molded) cabinet. Over the next several years, I noticed that product designs for the Apple computers actually did involve concepts that utilized the same horizontal motherboard installation, integral keyboard, and the top-mounted monitor that I'd initially applied to my first design. I wouldn't be arrogant enough to suggest that these features were survivors of my suggestions, but it is a thought that has often permeated my mind.

*****

I'd heard over time (from what source I do not remember) that Jobs had secured the support of a venture capitalist – or perhaps more accurately, a "finder" named Arthur Rock. Through this relationship, he and Wozniak had secured $25 million in funding. I'm not sure how the relationship developed, but it seemed that this partnership was the best possible fit on many levels, particularly because Arthur understood the fundamentals of a technology-based enterprise.

From my own personal business experience, I always found that whoever supplied the funding, usually had dominant control over the business, and more importantly over many product decisions. From what I was told about the relationship, Arthur seemed possessed of a superior understanding of technology-based enterprises. He appeared to recognize that such ventures were more prone to success if the corporate policies and product decisions remained in the hands of the product creators. For this reason, Arthur made certain that Jobs and Wozniak would jointly command a minimum of 51% of the voting interest in the corporation and its activities. I have no doubt that the subsequent successes of Apple stemmed directly from that division of voting rights. These events also explained the "why and how" of

110

the molded plastic cabinet. In my own defense, I would say that if I'd known about the financial holdings of Apple, my original approach to the cabinet design would have been much different.

It was several months later when I received a letter from a law firm containing a check drawn in my favor, in the amount of $1,500 to reimburse me for my brief efforts with Apple. Along with the check was a document that stated that if I accepted the money, I was formally relinquishing all interest in my previous 10% share of the Apple Computer Company. Considering that I had long since registered my abandonment formally with the Santa Clara County Registry Office, I regarded this unsolicited check as "found money," and willingly signed the paper as requested.

It is important to state that I forcefully dispute any misguided assumptions, on anyone's part that I was in any way deceived, defrauded, swindled or cheated out of my interest in the Apple enterprise. My separation from Apple was entirely of my own, well-considered decision, and one that was based on the facts that I had at the time. The question still remains, however, that if I'd known how the future would unfold, would I have so willingly abandoned my part in Apple? Answer: "Who knows?" One thing is certain: I consider it pointless to waste my tomorrows in meaningless hand wringing over "what might have been" if yesterday's decisions had been different.

Looking back on the events of that time – a span of nearly 35 years now – I cannot guarantee the accuracy of my memory, in regard to subtle details and minor circumstances relating to the origins of Apple Computer. Many events and happenings relating to the origin were actually outside of my personal experience. In fact, I cannot even recall whether my understanding of those origins came from Jobs directly or in combination with others. I can only speak with

Ron (left) with Apple co-founder Steve Wozniak (right), 2009

111

Ron (right) with Daniel Kottke, one of the earliest Apple employees, 2010

some certainty in matters of own personal involvement, and of happenings, and recollections of those events, as they were conveyed to me.

So to answer for the last time, "Did I make the right decision?" I have no idea, but there is this: while it is true that in all of my life I've never been rich; I've never been hungry either. In the days and years since my experience with the origin of Apple, I've totally "followed my own star," and pursued my own passion for product development.

In the process, I've been a compulsive inventor, and a seeker of projects that allowed me to have virtually complete control. I've been something of an anachronism at engineering (meaning out of place in time). My style of engineering for example, has followed the working environment (if not the monumental skills) of such nineteenth century engineers as Gustave Eiffel (who designed the Eiffel Tower), or John A. Roebling (who designed the Brooklyn Bridge). These men were super-engineers, whose engineering efforts positioned them at the pinnacle of a pyramid of other engineers, designers, draftsmen, and craftsmen who created their historic works. More importantly, there was no one in their related "pyramid" of designers and artisans whose job they couldn't do. Over the years I'd acquire skills as a draftsman, designer, illustrator, technical writer, machinist and lab technician, and was always at my best doing product development and wearing many hats. I delighted in carrying a development project from soup to nuts: formulation of the original concept, through product design and documentation, and hands-on prototyping, and even into production planning and development. This was the reason why I'd spent much of my adult life working at small companies, since they had limited resources and needed the versatility of skills that I possessed. In short, my work habits would simply not have been compatible in an enterprise as monumental as Apple.

*****

After my separation from the Apple company, I don't recall seeing Wozniak again for a number of years, but I did remain in casual contact with Jobs. We would go many months without speaking, and then out of the blue, I would get a call from him. It was many years later, for example, when Jobs phoned me with an invitation to attend as a VIP, and view his presentation of a new line of computers and monitors at a major computer show in San Francisco (I believe) in 2000. The arrangements on my behalf were exceptional on every level. I received roundtrip, first-class airline tickets to the event, and upon my arrival, Jobs' personal chauffeur greeted me and whisked me away to a luxury room at the Mark Hopkins Hotel. The following morning, Apple staffers picked me up at the hotel and drove me to the massive auditorium, where I was guided to a front-row seat. Immediately following his exceptional presentation, Jobs and I chatted for a few minutes, before giving me a brief walking tour of the convention. Afterwards, we went on a tour of the Apple facility and at the same time, joined Wozniak in the cafeteria for lunch. For the next hour and half, we dined and chatted around a small table on the patio. The entire lunch was a totally casual conversation, which was comprised of small talk and included pleasantries not amounting to any real substance. Then suddenly, it was over. We exchanged pleasantries, "Great seeing you again. Have a good flight back. Take care of yourself. Goodbye."

A quick limo drive to the airport and within a couple of hours, I was home again still wondering, "What the hell was that all about?" I concluded that it was simply a very kind gesture by Jobs and a chance for the three of us to get together again for old time's sake. It was indeed a most pleasant experience.

I didn't see Wozniak again until the Macworld Convention in San Francisco in 2008. It was a chance encounter and to be frank, I was quite astonished when he greeted me like a long-lost buddy (which, I suppose, I was.) With his characteristic enthusiasm, we spent several hours engaging in conversation, covering all kinds of newsworthy topics. To this day, he remains one of the most fascinating and gracious people I've ever known.

During the several personal contacts I had with Jobs over the years, he impressed me as a person who was laser focused on whatever he wanted to accomplish at any given moment. I still recall one chance encounter, which left me with mixed emotions. Shortly after leaving Atari (and after the takeover of Atari by Warner Communications) I landed a job with a very small engineering company called LDF Semiconductors. That was around 1977. The enterprise was a one-owner company that had developed a significant advancement in "Touch-Switch" technology. The owner had refined his circuit reducing it to a single miniature integrated circuit package. Moreover, he'd actually developed the application of his device so it could be used as a variable control, for such things as audio volume and moving a dot around a video screen. The user would simply slide his fingertip over a smooth, flat surface. This technology is most commonly used today as a virtual mouse or track pad in compact computers, laptops, and similar devices. In order to promote this Touch-Switch and variable control technology, LDF had set up a presentation booth at a computer technology convention. I was working at the booth when I was delighted by a visit with Nolan Bushnell and Al Alcorn (from my Atari days). I'm not sure about other visitors to the booth during the conference, but one of them may have included Jobs. Regardless, shortly after the expo Jobs contacted me. He wanted me to encourage my boss to sell the entire LDF Corporation to Apple. We had quite a lengthy and animated conversation over the issue, but in essence, my answer was not exactly what Jobs wanted to hear. I told him that, in my opinion, the LDF invention would simply be one component of the Apple product, but to my boss, it was effectively his entire life's work. As an alternate approach, I felt confident that an application license could be sold to Apple that would be exclusive within the field of computers, but I would not press my boss to sell off his entire company. We argued over the matter for some time, but I felt that the morality of the issue far outweighed Jobs' need for technological advances to the benefit of Apple. I firmly declined to plead his case, even though I probably would have been able to command a very substantial commission, if such a sale were actually to have happened. I don't think Jobs liked what I had to say about the issue, or the fact that I wouldn't help him.

Now over time, I've had considerable opportunity to rethink that exchange. And to be candid, I've come to regret my decision. I don't believe I was wrong in my opinion of the principles involved, but I now feel that I was wrong in not considering my boss's right to decide what he wanted to do for himself. However, as regretful as I am about my decision and my actions, the moving finger writes and having writ, gets a move on. If there's one thing I've learned about past choices and how to deal with them – particularly the ones we regret there's nothing one can do, except perhaps to learn from them. Lesson is: don't ever make the same mistake twice – except for those that are too much fun to make only once.

*****

In closing this discussion on my Apple experiences, though I would love to suggest that I was a dynamic force in the evolution of the Apple phenomenon, the fact remains that while that amazing story was playing out, I was actually off doing other, more mundane things. Even with such a limited involvement, it really was a fascinating experience to be that close to the vortex of the Apple story – to Steve Jobs, Steve Wozniak, and all the other people and events that came together to bring that amazing entity to life. Apple is truly a brand that has revolutionized the world and changed the way people communicate, how they process information, and indeed, how they live their lives.

PART VII
Then to Now

It was 1977, and my life over the next several years would be as casual and uneventful as one could imagine. I reignited a half-hearted attempt at running a stamp and coin business, and occasionally worked for short intervals at a few insignificant design/engineering jobs that effectively resulted in products of little significance.

Then as fate would have it, I received a strange phone call that would influence the next 16 years of my life. It seemed that my past life in the world of slot machines was about to rise up once again.

The phone call came from another Steve – Steve Abrams – the owner of an electronics manufacturing company called Thor Electronics in Salinas, California. He'd met with a woman who'd acquired an entire warehouse full of Centaur slot machines in various levels of operating condition, along with a large and random inventory of components. She was offering to sell the contents of the warehouse to Thor Electronics. Steve wanted Thor to acquire the lot in order to restore as many of the machines as possible to operating condition. The Nevada Gaming Commission had already qualified the product, so Thor could market this equipment at a substantial profit. Somehow, someway, Steve had learned I'd been the creator of these machines, and successfully tracked me down. He wanted to know two things: Did I think that such a venture was a good idea? And if so, would I be willing to take on the project?

Thor Electronics of California in Salinas, at that time, was quite a successful enterprise since its formation in 1966. They were primarily fabricators of commercial and military electrical cables and harnesses, but were also involved in the assembly of various kinds of equipment relating to the mainframe computer industry. Thor's largest customer, IBM, generated a gross

Inside of the Thor Vulcan slot machine

116

income of $40,000-$50,000 per week for the company building not only cables and harnesses, but also heavy-output power supplies and massive, large industrial computer disc drive memory units. Honeywell was their next largest client. The extent of Thor's operating facilities at that time included four large plants in California and Arizona, collectively employing more than 400 people. In fact, Thor's operations had been so successful that they were now able to undertake a more whimsical and adventuresome kind of business. The prospect of breaking into the gambling equipment industry seemed to appeal to them.

I was living in Canoga Park, California, in the San Fernando Valley at the time. It was a reasonable drive up to Salinas on a day in late summer of 1982. There I met with Steve and his brother, Jeff, to discuss the proposal over lunch. Before we'd even met, I had already considered Steve's offer very carefully, and my advice to the brothers had been systematically thought out. First of all, it had been 10 years since the Centaur fiasco had played out, and the warehouse – full of equipment that they had access to was not only well-aged, but had originally been put together by a management group that was more interested in stock manipulation than proper product development. This suggested that the products they built after I left the company were probably of questionable quality. And even though the Nevada State Gaming Commission had already qualified the equipment, the technology that I employed was unconventional, and any adventure into new equipment would be designed around more recent circuitry, such as TTL (Transistor-Transistor Logic) Integrated Circuits (a technology that I had already mastered). Moreover, the machines built under the Centaur name were mostly of the "Bar-Top" design that had a very limited market appeal. Their operation, as discussed earlier, simply involved dropping a coin into the slot. There wasn't even a handle to pull.

I suggested to the Abrams brothers that resurrecting the Centaur "ghosts" would be a costly move, and would yield only a limited chance at success and profitability. My recommendation (if they truly wanted a shot at the gaming equipment industry) was to essentially start over from scratch with a totally new design, organized around the currently popular TTL technology. It took a while for the men to come to a consensus regarding my suggestion. Over the years, I learned Steve's most pronounced characteristic was his capacity for procrastination, particularly when it came to significant business decisions. I often joked that he'd been a founding member of the

Procrastinator's Society (whimsically characterized as an enterprise that delayed until January 1988, in making their predictions for 1987).

After our meeting, Steve had promised to call me with his decision on the following Sunday. When he'd failed to do so by mid-afternoon of that day, I actually thought that the deal had fallen through. What's more, I was reluctant to call him because for me to do so would put me in a psychologically poor negotiating position.

Nonetheless, when 3:00 p.m. finally rolled around and there was still no call, I figured, "What the hell, why not!" Even at the outset of that call, I sensed that he hadn't yet made up his mind – until finally, in a fit of resignation, he told me to drive up to the office the following morning, and we'd put everything in place.

Once the Abrams brothers agreed to build a new product using the new technology, only one other problem stood in our way. At the time, California had very oppressive laws on the books concerning the possession of slot machines. For all practical purposes, under the current California anti-slot laws, it was effectively a crime to be in the same room with such a machine. These laws had been established in the late 1930s and were incredibly draconian. For example, the law states (and I am paraphrasing here) that it is a violation to possess or operate any machine that required the insertion of a coin for its operation that dispensed nothing of value, and operated in a manner that was unpredictable by the operator. In short, it was the perfect description of a pay telephone.

The way to circumvent these oppressive laws was simple. I immediately relocated to the Thor plant in Tucson, Arizona to establish operations there. I was provided with abundant shop space and all of the facilities I needed to develop our new product. This was also an excellent opportunity to hire my old friend Scott Bellairs to serve as my shop assistant – or effectively, a general dogs-body. I also hired a remarkably talented and ambitious young man by the name of Steve Harrison to work as my technical assistant. We were ready to begin! Not only did I have the complete facilities to properly create a new kind of casino machine, but more importantly, I had the support of people who were focused on producing a visionary and superior product for the marketplace.

The Vulcan Slot Machine Comes to Life

Thor Vulcan slot machine

The parameters for the new machine included a structure that was versatile enough to be assembled for either a three- or four-reel display, and the entire reels assembly would be removable for service as an integral unit from the front of the machine. Disengaging and sliding the top front panel upwards into a locked position would allow access to the interior section that wouldn't interfere with the machines on either side. A removable lower panel gave access to the hopper (coin payout unit). Finally, the electronics logic package was located beneath the hopper and behind the full-width coin tray. The circuit was even equipped to shift any "game in progress" into a standby mode, in the event of a power outage. This meant that the memory of the game status would hold until the game was completed, as soon as the power would be restored. The game was also designed to allow the player to buy from one to five lines of the displayed symbols. Finally, the entire system concept was organized to allow a range of game varieties to be assembled from an array of common sub-circuits and components. Even the game percentaging was alterable by convenient replacement of the reel symbol strips, and the corresponding PROM chips. The PROM, of course, is the "Programmable Read Only Memory" that carried the entire game parameters and awards.

Designing the newly named "Vulcan" slot machine was one of the most demanding development efforts I'd ever undertaken – and one of the most exciting. I always had the name "Vulcan" in the back of my mind as an evocative label for an electronic slot machine. The logo that I designed to go with the product was a *Flash Gordon*-esque replication of the Harley Davidson logo, but included the 1930s style lightening bolts (as a reflection of electronic operation). In effect, the final logo design fulfilled a childhood fantasy.

Best of all, the specifications of this project were perfectly suited to my work style. I had spent my entire life developing the skills needed to handle every aspect of a project of this kind, so that I was now supremely confident on the technical success of the entire enterprise. Over the next 18 months, with the help of my two assistants, the Vulcan slot machine came to life, evolving from a simple concept drawing into a complete, functioning product. Starting with the central logic package, I

Vulcan logo

personally designed and prototyped a functional logic that required nearly 200 IC chips in order to satisfy all of the operational functions. I then fabricated the mechanical reels mechanism that would be controlled by that logic package. These two principle assemblies were then combined with a commercial hopper (coin dispensing mechanism) to yield the complete operating structure of the game. The various sub-assemblies were housed within a rugged, casino-style enclosure. The attraction lighting, jackpot tower and sound were easily added later. To complete the final details of the machine, I drew up all of the graphic art, not only for the glass panels that glorified the front of the machine, but several complete sets of highly-stylized reel symbols as well. At last, Thor Electronics was ready to go into the slot machine manufacturing business – almost.

While I was beavering away at developing the product, the Abrams brothers had already applied to the Nevada State Gaming Control Board for all of the documents needed to apply for a Nevada qualified equipment manufacturing license. To further satisfy Nevada's licensing requirements, all of us were required to be individually licensed as principles in the newly formed Vulcan Corporation. Here is where the entire venture ran into serious roadblocks – not because of any personal or financial shortcomings –

but rather a consequence of Nevada's gaming development laws that evolved during the years of my absence from that industry.

Along with the licensing documentation from the Gaming Control Board, we also received a Product Qualification Document, which outlined the performance characteristics required for all new equipment to be considered for licensing. This document had been revamped and released several years before I'd joined Thor, back in September 1982. Nothing like this existed when I was involved in new product development years ago. To me, these new requirements were not only unexpected, but also rather shocking. The rules affecting the design of new product had shifted dramatically, and not for the better, in terms of the player. In order to understand the true impact of these new requirements, it's necessary first to take a short history lesson in the evolution of Nevada gaming.

*****

It all began back in 1931, during the depths of the Great Depression. Much of the U.S. at that time had been thrust into the hellish black hole of economic collapse, but Nevada fell into a deeper hole that had been growing for years. Nevada had nothing to start with, except Gila Monsters and sand fleas. To make things even worse, the price of silver, which had been the state's major mining resource, tanked at $1.25 per ounce. It was then that Nevada officials and some of the state's leading families got together to try and strategize ways to turn around their blistering sand heap of a state to bring in some measure of prosperity. Their efforts resulted in the enactment of two new and very significant laws. First, government officials reduced the residency requirements for the state to only six weeks, with the added feature that any resident could more conveniently obtain a legal divorce – with exceptional speed. The six-week residency requirement also promised handsome profits with its inherent linkage to the second law – the legalization of gambling. This law would give those who came to Nevada for a quick divorce something to do during their required waiting period. In fact, the combination of these laws succeeded beyond everyone's wildest expectations.

It wasn't long before state officials realized that if they wanted the new gambling laws to successfully enhance Nevada's prosperity, they would have to maintain an unblemished reputation for gaming integrity. The slightest hint of crooked gaming would cause Nevada's plan for prosperity to shrivel like a rotting vine. To fulfill this critical need for a sound reputation, the Nevada State Gaming Control Board was established under a system of regulations that would reflect the state's position of absolute "equal arbiter." This system stated that the clubs would

Ron with casino slot machines

not be allowed to cheat the players, and likewise, the players would not be allowed to cheat the clubs. A roulette wheel, for instance, has 38 little boxes, and the commission made certain that every wheel, in every club, have the exact same-sized boxes, and no trick devices or "gaffs" would ever exist to tilt the percentage in favor of the house. The commission also made certain that each facet of every dice was flat, parallel, square, and dimensionally true within less than one thousandth of an inch, and those dice had better not be weighted, or loaded. No deck of cards could be used in a casino that didn't conform to the rules of the commission. And finally, no latitude was given to any casino trying to break or bend the rules. Random inspections by plain-clothes investigators were a constant sight in casinos. If a club was caught with loaded dice, trick decks of cards, a gaffed roulette wheel, or any other flagrant violation, their license was gone forever and the owners would never again be licensed in the State of Nevada. As for gaming machines that were designed to emulate live table games (e.g., craps, blackjack, etc.), the playing odds of those machines had to be the same as the live table games that they were imitating.

The core principle of gaming, under the state's rules, dictated that the player had to be confident that the odds they were playing against were exactly as they appeared. For example, each die in a pair has six sides meaning that the possible number of combinations on a pair of dice was six times six, or 36. It followed that the odds against rolling "snake eyes" (1+1), was 1 in 36, or 35-to-1 against. The layout of a dice table is clearly marked as paying 30 to 1 for snake eyes on any single-roll bet. The commission concluded that the player is a mature adult, and if he's willing to accept a payoff of 30:1 when the odds against him are really 35:1, then he's at liberty to make that choice. The casino must be satisfied with the natural percentage of that take, and not try to "ginger-up" the odds in their own favor by slipping loaded dice onto the felt.

Slot machines were no exception. For starters, the Gaming Commission made no effort to set the payoff percentage "return to the player" of these machines. Instead they worked under the assumption that if the club got too greedy, their competition would soon drive them out of the business with more generous payoffs. In fact, if any club wanted to, they could put a machine in service with only one bar on each reel, leaving the remaining 19 spaces of each reel totally blank. They could then show an award chart that offered $1 for three bars on the pay line. All the club then needed to do was to find someone who would be willing to play such a machine. At the same time, state gaming inspectors could walk into any casino, unannounced, and demand that the Slot Manager open any machine. Recognizing that three sevens was normally the top winning combination, and that there was usually only one seven on each reel, the inspector could then order the man to set three-sevens on the pay line. (I'll leave to the reader's imagination the consequences if that test couldn't be passed.) Even more than that, each of the 20 stops on each reel had better be equally possible. If a casino manager couldn't demonstrate that the machine was capable of passing these tests, that club would likely be a warehouse by the following morning.

In short, the basic rules for gaming in Nevada were simple: "The player shall not be deceived, in any gaming activity, into thinking that he's playing against odds that are different from those that are visibly apparent."

That was the law when I was first involved in designing and building machines in the early 1970's. By the time Thor was ready to go into production, the Product Qualification Document had flagrantly revised this "gaming fairness" concept entirely.

*****

There were, in fact, well-founded reasons that influenced the commission's revision of the Nevada rules governing slot machine functional design. The basic slot machine mechanism had not materially changed since Charlie Fey's Liberty Bell machine in 1895. By the late 1960s, designers began to introduce the first electric and then electronic logics into the system. According to John Scarne's book, *A Complete Guide to Gaming* (1960), there were then 300,000 legal slot machines in the United States, mostly in the State of Nevada. There were also three million illegal machines operating throughout the rest of the country, mostly installed in the back rooms of roadhouses and in private clubs – roadhouses like the Arrow Club and Pettibone Club, just outside of Cleveland, Ohio. It would be a reasonable assumption that a substantial percentage of those illegal machines probably contained "gaffs" – that is, tended to seriously shift the normal odds of the game more heavily to the house's favor. These gaffs might have included what were called ten-stop reels. A normal reel would display 20 pictures and at the core of that reel was a twenty-toothed star. When the stopping-hammer fell, it would randomly engage one of the 20 available notches. However, in a ten-stop machine, each star only had 10 notches, so that half of the symbols shown on the reel could never appear on the pay line.

Then there were the machines that had the proper twenty-notch stars, but one or more of these notches would have a semi-circular bit of metal (called a bug) affixed to it, so that that particular symbol could appear only above or below the pay line, but never directly on the line.

Sometimes the gaff was as simple as mounting weights on the wheels so the symbols on one side would be less likely to stop on the pay line than those on the other side. There were even cases where certain points on the stars might be ground down or rounded off, while others were kept razor sharp, all to influence higher or lower probabilities of certain symbol positions over others.

To fully understand the implications of these tricks, you must appreciate exactly how the percentage (or take) of a slot machine really works. On a typical three-reel slot machine, each reel is designed to display one of 20 possible symbols. This means the total of all of the possible three-reel combinations is determined by simple math: 20 x 20 x 20, which equals 8,000 total combinations. The symbol distribution around the positions of the three reels is then arranged so that out of all of the 8,000 possible combinations, approximately 1,000 of these will be winners. What's more, the symbol distribution is also arranged so that each winning combination awards the player with an average of seven coins.

To determine the percentage the house takes on a machine, imagine that we might cycle through all 8,000 of the possible combinations, one combination at a time. In the process we will consider that each combination represents a single coin into the machine. This means when we have completed the total cycle of all 8,000 combinations, 8,000 coins will be paid into the machine. It also means that the cycling process will select the 1,000 winning combinations, and on average, pay seven coins back to the player. A complete cycling through all of the 8,000 combinations, therefore, will result in 8,000 coins played into the machine, and 7,000 coins returned to the player. By deduction, this means seven out of every eight coins played into the machine will be returned to the player – for a return of 87.5%. The house take on such a machine is 12.5% (which is actually quite a tight machine). Finally, any legal machine that is properly built (without gaffs) must be so constructed that its operation would be completely random. If so, such a machine might possibly hit three jackpots in a row, or it might go through thousands of plays before it hits again. That's the chance element of the game, and the kind of performance that makes such machines so evocative.

Over time, if the play on any particular machine is truly as random as it is designed, in the short run, it could make or lose a significant amount of money for the casino. The consequence of random averages over an extended period of time will guarantee the casino operator a very good living, particularly in a casino that is operating hundreds or even thousands of such machines. Such an array of machines simply grinds out the average percentages, as if the facility was an adding machine.

On one occasion, when I had a new machine on a field test, the casino manager at the old Mint Hotel & Casino in downtown Las Vegas told me, "If I had my way, I'd take all the roulette wheels, twenty-one tables and craps tables and throw them out in the alley, and put in more slot machines. The fact is, that on any given night, I can't say whether any particular table will make or lose $10,000. On any given weekend, I can tell within 5%, what the slot department will yield."

In the days of the old mechanical machines, when the slots may have been very successful for casino owners, there were plenty of serious issues they had to contend with, chiefly from the dishonest members of society called "slot cheats." In fact, among these was one particular group known as "cripple shooters." They were slot cheats who preyed on certain kinds of poor defenseless machines that had various types of problems – problems that made it difficult for them to defend themselves. In short, machines that had some kind of mechanical fault that worked in favor of the player, a slot cheat could exercise to his own advantage.

I remember a conversation I had with the slot manager at the Showboat Hotel, a man by the name of Roy Doyg, who called my attention to a typically-dressed, average looking sort of guy who'd just walked in the door.

Roy broke off our conversation with the casual comment, "Just a moment. I need some time to watch this guy."

I followed his lead, and for the next 20 minutes, I saw the visitor drift from one machine to another, spending extra time at certain machines. Finally he settled on a four-reeler, and played it for about 10 minutes before he headed to the cashier's cage to cash out his accumulated coins.

As soon as the man left the casino, Roy called over to one of his mechanics. "Hey George! Take machines 36, 421, and 187 into the shop. They've got some problems."

Roy had immediately recognized the fellow as a well-known "cripple-shooter" who worked a number of casinos in the area. I was somewhat surprised, as I asked, "Why didn't you bust the guy as soon as he came in?"

Roy's response was most instructive. "I couldn't do a thing like that. He works for us! He doesn't know he works for us, but he does. He tells my people very efficiently and very cheaply where all the bad machines are."

There were also more determined slot thieves who preyed on the casinos, often employing the most ingenious and amazing contrivances imaginable. For instance, a well known cheating method used an ordinary metal tape measure that had been modified with "kinks" at various points along its length. The tape could be inserted under the base of the machine and snaked into the machine so that one end would eventually reach into the timing clock mechanism. When the handle of a mechanical slot machine was pulled, the reels were kicked into spinning motion, while at the same time, a spring-loaded bar in the base of the mechanism was drawn back. As the bar returned, it executed all of the game functions in proper sequence. The return of this bar was slowed to a regulated speed by a mechanical clock, a mechanism much like the dial of an old dial telephone. This clock was positioned at the lower back of the internal mechanism. If the slot thief kinked the metal band at proper distances and shoved it under the base of the internal mechanism, it would eventually poke the gears of the clock and stop the travel of the bar. It was then simply a matter of watching for the right symbols to come into place, and alternately release and stop the clock causing the selected symbols to line up on the pay line. Instant jackpot!

All of the common mechanical machines during that time were equipped with a feature called an escalator, which was positioned just below the coin entry and across the top-front of the cabinet. The escalator displayed the last six to eight coins that had been played into the machine, so that floor security personnel could quickly spot anyone who might be playing slugs. When a coin was played into a machine, it would come to rest at the far left of the escalator window, in a position directly in front of the "firing pin." The firing pin was a short post designed to push outward as soon as the player started to pull the handle. If no coin was in position at the time of the handle pull, the continuing outward motion of the pin would tell the mechanism that no coin was in play, and would not allow the handle to operate.

If, on the other hand, a coin was already in position as the player started to pull the handle, this pin would be obstructed by the coin, and the handle would then be free to pull. The pull of the handle would then simultaneously drag all the coins in the escalator to the right by one position, leaving the left-hand coin space again empty, until another coin was inserted for the next game.

Here is how the sophisticated slot cheat could attempt to beat the machine. A relatively quiet electric motor was fixed to the back of the cheater's belt, outfitted with a flexible speedometer-type cable that ran up the sleeve of his left arm and was tucked away under his jacket. This cable ended with a miniature, right-angled drill-head that could fit inconspicuously into the palm of his left hand. Using his left hand, the cheat would insert coins into the coin slot, and at the same time, he would drill a hole in the cast-aluminum front-panel, directly in front of the firing pin. Finally, when the hole was complete, the cheat simply poked the end of a nail or paper clip through the hole to hold back the firing pin, so that he could then free-play the machine to his heart's content.

There was another type of cheater who was a bit more adventurous than the others, and worked machines with a dangerous trick. This crafty thief would reach up through the throat of the coin tray to the trap door under the jackpot box. By manipulating this trap door, he caused a few coins to fall out. That might not seem sufficiently profitable, from our present point of view, except that this variety of slot cheat invariably worked quarter or half-dollar machines, and if he was skilled enough, even dollar machines. Remember, at that time the slot machines contained all silver coins! It was a dangerous strategy, however, because if he became too aggressive, he might actually succeed in triggering the trap door, which operated under the influence of a very heavy spring. At that point, aside from the benefit of dropping the entire contents of the box, a very painful situation also might occur. To get around this problem, the cleverest of these slot cheats would fashion and wear specially shaped metal fingertips, meticulously colored to look completely life-like.

There was an incident, I recall, when one of these fellows was successfully working a machine's jackpot box, but unaware that the player sitting beside him was watching. The bystander thought this stunt looked like quite a cool trick, and soon started to jiggle the works of his own machine the same way. In fact, he was so successful that after a few moments, a resounding snap announced the triggering of the jackpot box trap door. That's when the machine – and the amateur slot cheat – both went to the hospital together.

There were even slot cheats who fashioned "jimmies" that were so sophisticated that they could actually get into the reels compartment to re-position those reels up or down (after the game had ended) in order to cause the jackpot symbols to line up on the pay line. They would then call an attendant, and claim a "no-drop" jackpot.

These were only a few of the scams facing the casino managers. A slot manager at the old Mint Hotel & Casino, in fact, once told me, "The one situation that really keeps me up nights, is the fact that I'm running a thousand machines out there on the floor. And between jackpot boxes, coin tubes and hoppers, there's an average of $50 in cash in each machine. That's $50,000 in completely uncontrolled cash on the floor, and there's damned little I can do to regulate it." (Incidentally, $50,000 back in those days was roughly equivalent to $1 million in today's money.)

These were just some of the concerns that virtually every casino and slot manager I'd met over the years had to deal with. I have no doubt that the decisions of the casino operators and the gaming commission was influenced by these nightmarish considerations, when the new micro-processor-based machines were introduced to the industry. These new systems had no mechanical clocks. The timing and functional sequence of all of the new machine's operations were then under the control of the electronic microprocessor logic.

Until the advent of the microprocessor machines, percentaging (how the earnings of the machine are established) was achieved entirely by the physical distribution of symbols on the reels – reels that were stopped entirely at random. Then, in effect, the machine "looked" at the reels to determine whether or not the resultant combination (on the pay line) was a winner, and if so, the award amount.

In fact, the openness of machine operation in those days meant that a focused player could probably see for himself how many pictures were on each reel, and possibly even the actual distribution of all of the symbols, so that a particularly observant player might possibly work out the actual "take" on the machine he was playing.

To this reality, add a fact that isn't commonly recognized by most people – that all of the energy that drives every action within an old mechanical slot machine is provided directly by the player as he pulls the machine's handle. In short, by its nature, the handle provided a direct communication to the player of the internal workings of such machines. In 1940, this curious combination of facts led to one of the most astonishing episodes in slot machine history.

The story is recounted in detail in John Scarne's book, *A Complete Guide to Gambling* (1960). It's the tale of a man by the name of Jake Kosloff who, in the days preceding World War II, suddenly showed up in the gambling Mecca of Las Vegas, bearing all the characteristics of an ordinary slot-playing tourist. Soon his playing habits proved to be truly extraordinary. Starting in one of the famous downtown casinos, he performed the remarkable feat of playing a machine until he'd succeeded in draining the coin tube and then hit the jackpot. Remarkably, he continued to casually move to another machine where he repeated the performance. It's unclear how many machines he attacked in this manner before he departed to another major casino where he duplicated these same achievements. By the time he'd left town (with a considerable haul of cash), his behavior had already attracted the attention of various casino managers, who took note to watch out for this fellow if he ever showed up again, which, of course, he did.

Sometime later Jake reappeared and proceeded at once to execute a repeat performance. This time, however, as soon as he'd left the first casino (with a substantial amount of their money), the slot manager immediately had his people carefully examine all of the machines that the man had been playing to see if any evidence of cheating could be discovered. Nothing irregular was ever found. Of course, word immediately went out to the other clubs' security teams who took careful note of Jake's actions. Yet the fact remained that nothing unusual was detected in Jake's behavior. He was simply playing the machines, like any common tourist – while at the same time, draining every machine of its coins.

I think it was the third or fourth club that Jake visited when security unobtrusively invited him to the casino manager's office. He was immediately searched for any possible possession of some kind of cheating device. Needless to say, nothing was ever found. The management made it very clear from the start that they had no evidence to accuse him of slot cheating, but at the same time they were particularly anxious to know, "What the hell he was doing?"

Jake's response was particularly shocking. He informed his interrogators that he could beat any machine in the place. After nearly half a century of profitable slot operations, the management had serious doubts about Jake's claims, but after a short while, the discussion ended with (as it was reported) a $10,000 bet. It was a chance for the club to get their money back, suggested Jake. To enable this remarkable slot-man to demonstrate his point, a brand new Mills High-Top machine was uncrated and dutifully loaded with quarters. Jake began at once to play the machine in a most casual manner, while carrying on an equally casual conversation with his hosts, until at one point in his monologue he blurted out, "Two cherries."

Immediately thereafter, as the spinning reels stopped, the first two reels displayed cherries on the pay line. As surprising as this event was, the conversation continued. Then a few minutes later, the man said casually, "Three oranges." And just as predicted – click, click, click and three orange symbols lined up on the pay line. Finally, it wasn't long after that when Jake called "Jackpot" to announce in advance, as the three black bars clicked onto the line, and the silver horde crashed into the tray.

The witnesses stood in amazement by what they'd just witnessed, and it took them several moments to recover. The slot manager conceded the bet, but with one provision, "We'll pay the bet, of course," he began, "but you've got to tells what you're doing."

At that point in time there was no doubt that the slot machine had become the backbone of the gaming industry. Nor was there any question that if Jake could beat the game, in time many others would do so as well.

Jake explained that he'd recently left a job with Mills, the company who built the machine that he had just performed his "magic" on. During his employment, he learned the distribution of every reel-strip combination that Mills produced. He'd also learned simultaneously how to master the art of the handle pull. If the handle pull was light, the reel spin would be relatively slow; a firm pull would cause the spin speed to increase. He had discovered that this technique could be used in combination with the constant timing of the mechanical clock to execute a method he called "rhythming." By this method, in combination with the ability to precisely tell time (in seconds) in his head, he could cause the reels to stop sooner – or later. Then during normal play, he could apply this combination of skills and knowledge to cause desired symbols to accurately come to rest on the pay line – just by "playing" the machine – without any tricks or devices.

For a brief time after this episode, as the word spread of Jake's remarkable skills, the leaders of the industry began to fear the end of the slot machine, and a huge dent in gaming revenues. Technology would not allow such a happening to occur. The discovery of the rhythming method – and the elements that made it possible – soon led to the invention of a slot machine component called a variator, which automatically changed the starting position of the timing bar to irregular positions after each game. This innovation solved the immediate problem, but at the same time, left a haunting fear of what other tricks might be possible with the continuing run of "mechanical" machines.

The microprocessor-based slot machine put an end to all of these concerns and alleviated many other fears at the same time. For example, coin spillover from the mechanical machines dropped coins, at random, into a collection box within the game's pedestal (called the house hole). The problem with this approach was there was no way of knowing how much coinage was in this box at any point in time, at least not until that box got into the counting room. This left the club vulnerable to sticky-fingered technicians and box-collectors, as well as many other kinds of pilfering. With the new electronic machines, every coin paid in or out of a machine would be metered, so that the counting rooms would know well in advance precisely how much coinage would be in each drop box before they arrived.

The new electronic machines also offered perfect solutions to the problem of cheats who jimmied the wheels after the game was over so they could turn a "near miss" into a no-drop jackpot. The first approach added sensors to the mechanism that would detect the slightest reel motion at time between games. The ultimate answer was something called the "virtual reel" concept. In this final system (now universally employed), percentaging was no longer done on the physical reels, but rather within the electronics of the machine. The logic package in today's machines contains high-speed "electronic" reels that supposedly stopped at random, and this electronic core signals the physical reels to command them where to stop! It was that final innovation that inevitably led the entire Nevada gaming industry to a fatal revision of their original rules – rules that had previously assured equal representation of the interests of both the casinos and gaming public.

The advent of the virtual reel system immediately influenced an entirely new line of thinking in game psychology. When there were only 8,000 possible combinations in the play of a game, it was impossible to design a game that could pay out more than 1,000 coins for any winning combination. Players would be more tempted to play a game in which the highest award would be 10,000 or even 100,000 coins. How about a nickel machine that could offer $100,000 jackpot? The only way to accomplish that, of course, was with a machine that offered 100 million possible combinations – and now with the virtual reel system that capacity was immediately available. When the game's electronic reels determined where the physical reels were supposed to stop, those electronic reels weren't limited to the 20 stops that appeared on the physical reels. In fact, at the present time, virtually every electronic slot-machine that exhibits physical reels with 20 stops, the internal, electronic reels contains nearly 256-stops, yielding in excess of 16-million possible combinations. The reader can then work out for himself the number combinations which would result from a four-reel machine – which then multiplies that 16-million combinations by another 256 times.

That's when the system broke. The new Nevada rules that resolved the number of accounting and performance problems, now demanded that all new machines contain microprocessors. In so doing, contrary to their original gaming philosophy, the state now demanded that machines can only be qualified if they "deliberately deceive the player into believing he's playing against one set of odds," when in fact the odds against him were greater by many orders of magnitude. In effect, under the new rules of the game, the house was dealing the hand in the back room and told the player, "Sorry, you lose!"

Under the rules that were in place when I'd been building machines in early 1970s, a virtual-reel slot machine would have been unlicensable, as a "gaffed" game. Moreover, the new electronic gaming systems would be the perfect example of the old adage that "nothing comes without a price." So it is that the wonderful new system that seemed to solve all the casino's security problems, and enabled the profitable offering of spectacular jackpots, also exhibited inherent and built-in weakness, which over time would cost the industry billions of dollars in revenue.

*****

It's important to remember that in the design of mechanical slot machines (or even electrical machines for that matter), every aspect of the game's operation was totally observable. Any skilled inspector, for example, could spot a mechanical gaff instantly, or even trace electric circuitry with considerable ease. In the design of my own machines, for example, I was performing electronically, what had previously been accomplished mechanically using widgets, levers, cams and springs. Yet my machines (like the mechanicals) left the reels free spinning, and stopped them by a totally random timer means using a time base with a continuously shifting rate of change. Also similar to the mechanical machines, once the reels had been stopped, my system literally "looked" at the symbols on the pay line to detect a possible winner, and would then determine the count of coins to pay out. What's more, the physical circuits that were placed into my machines reflected the exact schematic designs that were filed with the

Gaming Commission for approval. Any skilled tech could quickly discover if my physical circuits differed in any way from the diagrams that I submitted. This inherent detectability, in fact, had been standard in the licensing of every gaming machine before the advent of the microprocessor-based gaming technology.

The problem with the new microprocessor system, as compared to its predecessors, is that the inner workings are practically "invisible." Prior to the microprocessor, machines had mechanical parts or a combination of circuit components for every individual function of the system. In other words, previous game functions were all based on hardware, which was directly observable. A microprocessor, on the other hand, is a "software" system. That is, the entire game and all of its functions are established in a software program, a program that is packaged entirely within a single integrated circuit chip – the PROM. If anyone tried to "read out" that program, all they could find was an endless string of ones and zeroes, the functions that are only known by the people who wrote that program. In short, there's nothing for an inspector or technician to see. The innards of the machines contained an electronic package that consisted of a microprocessor "brick," and a program "brick," where two wires ran off to the handle and the other wires ran off to the coin acceptor, to the hopper (coin dispenser), etc. The program, logic, and the "tricks" of the game (if any) are undetectable by anyone!

*****

To better understand the price that the gaming industry was now obliged to pay for "security" and other assumed advantages gained by microprocessor-based equipment, consider the following theoretical event.

On an ordinary day, during an ordinary week, a very ordinary looking middle-aged guy walks into a typical casino in downtown Las Vegas. He buys a roll of quarters and saunters around the casino sampling various machines until his coins are depleted. Then he returns to the cage for another roll. Finally, about half an hour (and two rolls of quarters) later, he settles on the megabucks machine and starts to seriously play the game. After about 40 minutes or so, the spectacle begins. There's bells, whistles, flashing lights, and everything but fireworks. Everyone in the casino turns to see what's going on and is captivated by the spectacle. Soon the Slot Boss and the Casino Manager, along with security, appears on the casino floor. You can easily spot the security guys because they're the ones with one solid eyebrow across the face, and Band-Aids on their knuckles (because they drag on the pavement).

A giant flashing number has appeared across the top of the machine's billboard: $10,000,000."

You can't hear yourself think over the shouts, screams, bells and whistling. The fellow has hit the "big one." A call is immediately put in to the Gaming Commission, who dispatches staff to the casino within minutes. The machine is opened by security and the heart of the game's logic package – the PROM (programmable memory that holds every detail of the game) – is extracted. People from the Gaming Commission bring a duplicate PROM, and a piece of equipment called a comparetor, just to verify that the factory-supplied program hasn't been switched or altered. Within an hour, all of the testing has been successfully completed, and our rather ordinary man is handed a certified check for his $10 million – that is, after he's filled out his W4-G form for the IRS.

So what might actually have happened here? Simply this. Our ordinary, middle-aged guy might well have been a second cousin to the fellow who'd actually written the program in the first place! That program may have included a non-standard sub-program embedded within it. A sub-program that really has nothing to do with the normal play of the game, but everything to do with the win.

The trick was simple. Our "player" may have made a series of sequential bets, on this five-coin game. He might have started by betting three coins on a game, and on the next game, three coins again. Then in the subsequent games, his bets, included 1 coin, then 5 coins, then 2 coins, then 2 coins, then 3, 3, 5, 5, 1, and then 3 – (or any similar sequence of bets that one might imagine), to form a sequence of game bets that were pre-programmed for the machine to recognize. After that specific sequence of game bets, he started the final game by betting five coins.

That was when the logic woke up and said, "Oh. Now I'm supposed to hit five-sevens Super-Jackpot!"

Such a sub-program might have been written into the game two years earlier, and now it was time for "cousin" to cash in. Worse yet for the gaming industry, there was no possible way for anyone to know – or

135

even discover the scam. There was an added string of indecipherable digits (ones and zeroes) within the game chip that made up a trick sub-program that was already pre-loaded (like a mole) into the original game. Whether speculation or fact, serious suspicions on the part of game builders, as well as the industry overall led the product manufacturers to take additional precautions. One of the most unusual precautions was an effort to break up the program writing activity so it was performed by several compilers. Of course all that did was to force the loot to be split more ways.

The reader must understand that the scam I've just described, while purely speculative, is only one of countless schemes that may have bilked the casinos out of billions over the past few decades. The state of Nevada lost uncountable millions in revenue – all in direct consequence of microprocessor based gaming machine technology.

*****

This significant violation of Nevada's original philosophy regarding the casino-player relationship was direct evidence that an unholy alliance had been established between the casino owners, the gaming equipment manufacturers, and the Nevada State Gaming Control Board to populate the state with gaming machines that possessed odds that would never be accessible to players. Faced with this new reality, and with other aspects of the new gaming machine qualification rules that were just as egregious, neither Steve nor I wanted to participate further with this project.

Even though Thor had invested more than $150,000 in this development effort, Steve suggested that we "put it on the shelf," which we both knew was a euphemism for, "the end."

While I was deeply disappointed that once again, circumstances foiled my efforts at a serious involvement in the gaming equipment industry, the exercise had earned me the respect of the Abrams brothers for my demonstrated skills and ability.

Armed with that confidence, the brothers presented me with a new serious engineering task. I immediately moved back to Salinas, California, and was installed as chief engineer at the Thor plant.

The new project focused on the company's transition into military cable and connector technology. It seemed that a major military-electronics manufacturer (Litton Data Systems) in Southern California had created a miniaturized universal field computer, principally for use by the United States Marine Corp. It was a highly ruggedized device not only suited to various immediate applications, but also had the potential for a broad spectrum of additional uses in future development over a span of several years. However, a critical element of this miniaturized equipment, was the parallel creation of a family of micro-miniature electrical connectors, and the very demanding cabling technology that related to the connector system. The centerpiece of this development activity was a push-pull plug and receptacle set that would carry 37 pins, all packaged within a diameter of roughly three quarters of an inch. The connector set was keyed so when it was properly oriented, it was only necessary to push the plug into the receptacle until it clicked into the mated state. This plug also featured a coupling ring, which allowed the plug and its related socket (receptacle) to readily separate when pulled back. Pulling on the cable without retracting the coupling ring would not allow separation to occur, even under a force of 50 pounds or more. At least that was the original plan. The development of this connector set was agreed to be a joint effort between Litton, Thor, and a company by the name of Minicon, who held the patents on the very special connector pins.

On my first day in the Salinas office, I received the complete set of drawings for both the plug and the receptacle. At the same time I discovered a very serious problem. It seemed the connector sets worked very effectively, and not only performed the proper engagements and disengagements, but were also very tolerant to the abusive conditions in terms of environment and handling. Battlefield conditions, after all, are not kind to any type of high-tech equipment. These connectors and their related cables were required to demonstrate endurance to salt spray, altitude, shock, vibration and UV radiation, along with exposure to chemical and biological contamination, and the related de-contamination chemical baths. In effect, the military requirements covered everything but endurance to Aqua Regia and nuclear detonation (though I don't know how they missed those.)

In fact, this new product actually met all of those requirements, except for an intermittent problem. In fact, a specimen had been left on my drawing board, no doubt to tantalize me. It was an actual Litton computer module, with one of the new plugs engaged into its socket. After fiddling with it for some time, I finally concluded that the plug absolutely refused to separate from the receptacle, and probably wouldn't do so even if I used blasting powder. My first thought was that there might have been something wrong with the basic design. On this assumption, I began with a detailed analysis of this very clever mechanism before I finally discovered that the problem was intermittent. In fact, the reliability of the mechanism approached 98%. To the average person, that level of reliability might sound acceptable, but in a combat situation, any kind of equipment failure can be disastrous. When I focused on the intermittent nature of the fault, I realized that an analysis of dimensional tolerances would yield the answer I needed.

For the benefit of those who are unfamiliar with the production of machined parts, it is practically impossible for any machinist (or machining set up) to cut any machined dimension perfectly to a specified number. For this reason, dimensional allowances are provided, for each dimension of every component, as part of the design process, such as +/- 0.002 inches. The trick to finding the proper tolerance specification is to set the tolerances of all dimensions, precisely enough to assure that the assembled mechanism will always work. At the same time, this need for precision must be relaxed enough so that manufacturing doesn't become too costly.

It was during this overall analysis that I discovered that if the specific dimensions of certain parts went to the wrong tolerance extremes, it became possible for one particular part to become wedged, in such a manner to make it impossible for the connector set to separate.

All I had to do was to tighten the numeric values of certain tolerances for a few critical dimensions, and the problem vanished entirely. In the decade-plus that followed, Thor produced several tens of thousands of these plugs and receptacles, along with the related cable assemblies for the U.S. Military. Yet, throughout the operating life of this product line, including extensive service in the first Gulf War in 1990, you could count on the fingers of both hands, the total number of connector set failures in products using this design.

My success in solving the connector-set problem, essentially secured my on-going employment with Thor for the next 15 years – all the way to the point of my self-elected retirement (or what I thought was my retirement) in 1998. This run of employment not only turned out to be the longest, but also the most satisfying of my entire career, at least to that point in time.

Among the features of my employment at Thor that perfectly suited my style, was that it allowed me to be involved in every phase of a product's development, from fashioning the initial concepts, to design and creation of the first prototypes, to the establishment of production documentation and tooling, and even hands-on fabrication of custom equipment for use in production, qualification and product testing. I also took pleasure in the extensive travel that came with the job, principally for customer interface and visiting the facilities of suppliers. Steve Abrams would make sure we always traveled in style and made certain we identified the best restaurants in the area before we arrived. Best of all, there was always something new happening, and different for me to do. I often compared it to feeling like a mosquito in a nudist colony, hardly knowing what fun job to attack next.

My attitude towards my employment at Thor was best indicated by one particular incident, when Steve came into the office on a Sunday and asked me, "What the hell are you doing here?"

On that occasion I recall telling him, "What else should I be doing? Sitting around my apartment, listening to my arteries harden?"

I was simply living a philosophy that I'd often expressed to others, "Find a job that you enjoy so much that you'd be happy doing it for nothing, and you'll never work a day in your life." My job at Thor was such a delight that I regularly spent seven days a week in the office; Sundays and holidays never meant time off to me.

I do have to admit there was a period that my "perfect job" wasn't so perfect. This particular interval put a real crimp in my style. It was over a period of nearly three years, when the company became the victim of their main customer, IBM. The problem didn't suddenly appear, but rather evolved over a long span of time. Decades earlier, IBM has been the virtual originator of an outside labor system called "farm-out." This labor utilization method was developed when IBM began its most massive growth – immediately before, during and after World War II. The company had grown so large, in fact, that their engineering, designing, drafting and management offices, as well as their record-keeping and inter-departmental staff, along with the related facilities, became so burdensome that they could no longer support the "internal" cost of "in house" manufacturing. At one point, IBM's supporting staff and facilities actually drove their internal "labor costs" as high as $150 per hour. Under that kind of financial burden, they literally couldn't afford to manufacture much of anything within their own walls. It was then that IBM pioneered this profoundly successful manufacturing strategy called "farm-out."

Under this system, the company subcontracted virtually all of their physical manufacturing needs to hundreds of small suppliers and labor shops around the country. These shops received drawings, worksheets, and supporting documentation from IBM for the assembly of equipment, sub-assemblies, cables, wiring harnesses, or whatever. Then during carefully structured negotiations, they accurately determined how many man-minutes of labor would be needed to fabricate a particular product or sub-assembly, and what rate per minute would be charged for labor back to IBM. By utilizing this strategy IBM could establish – to the penny – exactly what each product would cost, and therefore, exactly how much they could charge for it. This was particularly important when they were marketing their products in competition with enterprises like Honeywell, Westinghouse and GE. They could sell their products for marginally higher than what they were paying to have them fabricated and shipped, but at the same time, at prices that would marginally under bid the competition. It was as simple as that – and it worked!

During the first decade of this practice, IBM found the technique hugely successful and they became extremely protective of their outside labor sources. They took great pains, for example, to be certain that their suppliers made money and the business base of their suppliers was sound. IBM looked for companies that diversified and didn't depend on more than half of their business revenues from IBM. This parental relationship encouraged the potential labor force to heavily compete with each other for a slot among the IBM labor suppliers, particularly since IBM paid them like a slot machine. The supplier delivered the product, and had their invoices honored within days.

From the earliest days of Thor Electronics in 1966, IBM had been their most reliable client. Turning over as much as $50,000 a week, Thor produced equipment wiring harnesses and interconnection cables, as well as providing assembly labor for various types of supporting equipment that was used in very large, main-frame computers. To Thor, it was a dream relationship with IBM. This kind of business format was called "build-to-print." IBM would supply all of the engineering, designs and drawings, and at the same time, IBM supplied the raw materials directly, or involved themselves in a three-way relationship among IBM, Thor and the materials suppliers. This latter approach was done in such a way that Thor could buy the needed materials at huge quantity discounts that far exceeded levels that might otherwise would have been possible if Thor had not been buying under IBM's avuncular wing.

This close business relationship had been in force for well over 15 years, when an IBM project came in the door that was unlike anything Thor had ever done for them. It was the mid 1980s and IBM Purchasing had only recently learned of Steve's newly acquired engineering capability – namely, me. As IBM saw it, this new capacity – a capability that Thor had never exhibited before – fit well with the other facilities in Thor's grasp. IBM's other suppliers did not offer these full-range activities. Thor not only now possessed, a full-range machine shop and a complete qualification-testing laboratory, but possessed four huge Wabash rubber molding presses as well. Together with the design and development services that I could offer, these capabilities made Thor an almost unique source for complete neoprene-molded power and signal cables any size and virtually any complexity – cables that could be custom fabricated. Even the tooling for the molded connector terminations would be turned out in our own machine shop.

It seemed IBM had run into a problem with a connector supplier, who'd been providing them with quantities of a rather massive connector set for nearly 20 years. It was a huge, three-phase connector set, used as the primary power source for their mainframe industrial computers. Over the preceding 24 months, this supplier (for whatever reason) had been inching up their prices on both the Plug and mating Receptacle until it finally reached an intolerable level. Having apparently approached the limit of their patience, the IBM Purchasing Department asked Thor to quote the development of a completely new, neoprene-molded connector set – a connector set that would have significant technical advantages over the original supplier's products. For instance, the original product was not molded to the cable, but mechanically assembled. The cable-clamp that anchored the mechanical assembly to the cable proper was secured with heavy screws, with the ends that projected at least an inch to either side of the plug shell. I found this rather hazardous detail to be very strange, since the product carried both the UL (Underwriters Laboratories) and

CSA (Canadian Standards Association) certifications. These agencies (to my surprise) had effectively expressed satisfaction with the product's general safety, in spite of such an obvious a "personal injury" hazard. IBM had requested that new product be completely inter-changeable with the original plug and receptacle – that is, the product would need to perfectly mate with both the plug and receptacle from the earlier manufacture.

From the start, IBM readily funded every penny of this product development activity, from mold fabrication, to engineering time, to the prototyping of all the components. What made this project so tempting to Thor was the obvious implication that when we completed development, Thor would essentially be the sole supplier of mainframe power cables and mating receptacles for all IBM mainframe computers, as long as they continued to supply these products at a reasonable price.

From the beginning, this project advanced with remarkable speed and efficiency, and within three weeks the entire product (plug and receptacle) was fully engineered, and prototype components were fabricated, ready for assembly and for the molding of the first cable. In parallel with this effort, appropriate liaison had been formally established with both UL (Underwriters Laboratories) and CSA, whose qualifications were required before IBM would accept delivery of the finished products. It was a curious fact, however, that while Thor had been producing fabricated wire harnesses and connector-mounted cable assemblies for decades, all bearing UL labels, Thor's only relationship with UL had been Thor's commitment to using only UL approved wire, cable ties and related components. In effect, Thor had never previously been certified as an UL-qualified manufacturer. The new molded power cable was a different animal altogether, and the molding process then made "manufacturer's qualification" essential.

Strangely enough, from the time that the first molded cables came off the presses, it was a mere seven weeks before Thor successfully obtained certification from CSA (Canadian Standards Association). What's more, in order to be confident that we had planned for a top-quality product, for example, I had specified the same Military Standard neoprene that had been used in the manufacture of cables for the U.S. Marine Corps. Obviously, CSA thought this material was a good choice, or they wouldn't have approved the product. However, UL was playing an entirely different game altogether. Everything about the design and fabrication of our product was completely acceptable, but they claimed that our neoprene could not tolerate their "flame test." We tried the same test ourselves, and could not make the material hold a flame, once the torch was removed. Nonetheless, their conclusion remained unchanged. Our neoprene was not acceptable.

My immediate comment to them was, "Fine. Just tell us what neoprene you want us to use, and we'll use it!"

Their response was no less enigmatic than their complaint. "It's not our policy to tell people how to make their products." The result: a cast iron impasse. We had hit an impassable brick wall.

On the assumption that the reader has never been involved directly with UL, the shadowy legal relationship of UL with the products you buy may seem strange. The fact is that there is NO actual legal requirement to obtain UL qualification, either as a manufacturer, or for certification of the products. The problem is that if you manufacture any kind of product of an electrical nature that involves a voltage greater than 24 volts or (certain other products in different categories), and you don't have these products properly certified, no commercial distributor or commercial user will buy or handle your products. The simple reason for this is something called Product Liability Insurance. The fact is that UL is effectively the testing laboratory for the entire insurance industry. Product Liability insurance protects the distributor or marketer of products against lawsuits in the event that the end user should have any kind of nasty experience with that product. In short, if it's not UL registered, marketers won't sell it – and in the case of these cables – IBM wouldn't buy it. Moreover, the UL has only one allegiance – the insurance companies. The net result is three things. First, UL qualification is extremely complicated and expensive to obtain. Second, they will not be rushed even if your product is needed to prevent the end of the world, and third, they don't give a damn whether you ever get qualified or not.

For the next 16 months, Thor haggled and negotiated with UL and jumped through their hoops before we finally were able to obtain a UL listing on the cable product. That's when the bottom fell out. Now that we were in a pre-sprinting position to start mass-producing IBM's cables, the company informed Thor that the original supplier had suddenly "readjusted" its prices to a level that was acceptable to IBM. They wouldn't need our cable after all. It wasn't until then that we realized that the entire process had been nothing more than an elaborate scheme. IBM had simply used Thor as a "stalking horse" to force the original supplier to drop their prices! The fact that the Thor product was better and safer meant nothing – quality and safety be damned.

This exercise in futility was only the beginning of our deteriorating relationship with IBM. Something happened to cause a monumental shift in IBM's philosophy regarding their suppliers. It seemed that for decades the corporate profit margins of IBM had been steadily rising at the rate of about 5% per year. Over an interval of about 20 months, those margins declined. The company's new CEO and board of directors came to recognize that profit growth was no longer possible from the sales side of their business. In their view, this situation demanded a new policy to receive their future profit growth from the supplier's side! This meant that IBM had to simply pound down their supplier's margins.

At one point, I actually witnessed the direct effects of this new policy. As previously stated, it had been the practice for IBM and their suppliers to negotiate the labor rates for the coming year. Contrary to the practice of proceeding decades, in the two-year span that had just passed, I watched that labor rate drop from 23 cents per minute to 18 cents. I happened to sit in one of the most recent negotiations and witnessed something I'd never seen before. The two IBM reps who came to our offices couldn't have been older than 25 – which, in my opinion, was no justification for their arrogance and bad manners. The term "negotiation" in fact, really didn't mean anything. They simply demanded that the rate for the upcoming year would be 16 cents, and then confronted Steve with a whole list of "policy changes." I won't burden the reader with the details, other than to say these changes all involved shifting the expenses (previously absorbed by IBM) to Thor. It was bad enough that these negotiations amounted to nothing more than "take it or leave it," but their entire manner towards Steve was one of an over-bearing boss, chastising an errant employee. During that meeting, only my superhuman restraint kept me from blurting out something like, "You kids ought to be spanked!"

It was 1986, and until that moment, Thor had enjoyed a very successful and profitable relationship with IBM for the last 20 years. Suddenly, Steve was effectively confronted with either accepting the new rules of the game, or lose a turnover of roughly $45,000 per week. He reluctantly accepted the new terms of the agreement. From that day forward, the atmosphere around Thor darkened significantly, until one day later that same year when the staff was called into the front office for an announcement. Steve had spent the previous week doing an in-depth corporate audit that had suddenly revealed a desperate situation: Thor was $1 million in debt. In effect, they'd been wrapping a five-dollar bill around every wiring harness as it went out the door. Finally, in desperation, he'd notified IBM that very morning that unless they came up with $190,000 immediately, he would close the doors and IBM would be shorted nearly a $250,000 worth of products that would never be delivered. IBM actually did put the money into Steve's hands within 24 hours, but, of course, Thor Electronics became persona-non-grata.

By this time, word had rippled through the industry that IBM had implemented their new supplier's policy across the board. Not only had this policy posed a real threat to Thor, but literally hundreds of other IBM suppliers were falling over in rows like dominos, so many, in fact, that IBM was having difficulty finding anyone who wanted to do business with them any more. Among other strategies to alleviate their consequent supply problems, IBM moved to set up a "maquiladora," a plant in Mexico (supposedly the word on the street) to turn out a broad range of products at labor costs far below what they'd been paying to "farm out" people in the U.S. Unfortunately, the product "drop-out" (scrap) rate had apparently proved so high that IBM was forced to close the plant within a year. I had heard that IBM lost $25 million on that exercise.

Next (again from the word on the street), the company tried to build an entire "company town" in the desert, about 50 miles outside of Tucson. This scheme as well, it seemed, turned out to be yet another massive misjudgment. In time this strategy also proved to be more costly than profitable. When the market crash hit in 1987, the effects of IBM's disastrous supplier policies really came home to roost and were splashed on the business pages for everyone to see. The devastating effects of those policies had so profoundly contributed to the general dysfunction of the company that IBM's stock dropped from about $150 per share to nearly $45. Worse than that, while other stocks that were also hammered in the 1987 crash tended to fully recover over the next 12 to 18 months, it would be years before IBM would be able to approach its former level of credibility. Among other things, labor shops that had previously flocked to IBM continued to

145

shun them like a plague. How IBM ever recovered from the hole they'd dug for themselves, I was never able to discover. The effects of their foolishness on Thor and its staff would drag on for years.

Fortunately, Thor still had a modest base of other customers. One of the largest clients was the Naval Air Warfare Center located in Indianapolis. They were the primary buyers of the Litton field computer cables and other peripheral and accessory products for the U.S. Marine Corps, yielding seven-figure annual contracts for Thor. Another top client was a company called U.S. Windpower, a major operator of wind farms in California and other states as well. This wind-energy facility was one of the few who actually designed and built their own towers. Thor possessed the large Wabash rubber-molding presses making them a very marketable supplier for these kinds of ruggedized cables so commonly used by the U.S. military and environmentally demanding customers, such as U.S. Windpower. Because of this client base, Thor was able to generally recover from the very costly beating it had taken from IBM, although it was fully two to three years in the process.

The tragic part of the IBM experience was the colossal contraction in Thor's operating base. All three of the outlying plants were closed, and the former staff of over 400 people throughout the company was trimmed to less than 100. Those who remained with Thor were essentially the operating force of the main plant in Salinas, which continued actively to supply the needs of the clients we still retained.

*****

One experience, during my tenure at Thor, turned out to be my crowning achievement in the field of engineering. As stated earlier, the work we'd been doing for Litton (and the Naval Air Warfare) essentially involved a series of specialty cables related to the company's custom field computer. Over a number of years, the Marine Corp. had found many unique applications for the Litton device, and each of these applications demanded the development of a special cable just for that function. During the time of the Gulf War, if memory serves, there were up to 15 different cables in service by the military. In terms of supply and logistics, that's one weighty bunch of cables

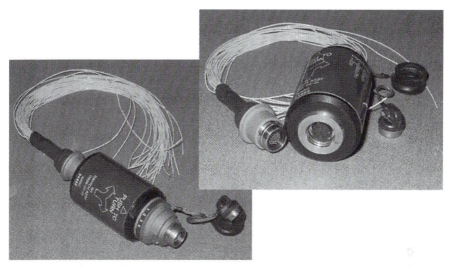

In-Line Cable Selector Switch Ron designed for Naval Air Warfare while at Thor

one weighty bunch of cable to ship globally to support the substantial number of these relatively tiny computer modules. Naval Air Warfare, in consequence, was determined to reduce this bulk by replacing four of the most commonly used cables with a single one. This single cable would be used in conjunction with a very sophisticated "in-line" switch. Instead of plugging the common cable directly into the computer, it would be plugged into one end of a special cylindrical switch – a switch that was roughly the size and shape of a small soup can. (We called it the hand grenade). The switch would then be plugged into the computer. An outer sleeve of this switch (like the shell of a can) rotated into positively stepped positions, around the core of that switch, with each position selectively performing the function of a unique cable. The net result was four very bulky cables would be replaced with a single cable and our custom selector switch.

It was a clever solution to the problem, but the development of the project itself also possessed a few unique problems. The purchasing officer at Naval Air Warfare Center decided to implement a new procedure for the government's acquisition of this switch. This officer apparently fancied himself a sufficiently competent engineer to undertake the design of the product himself and even execute the complete set of manufacturing (component) drawings. Thor (and a few other suppliers) was given an RFQ

147

(request for quotation). Under this RFQ, we were required to bid on this device in a quantity of 3,000 units, and execute the bid in conformance with the design and details presented to us. The man's design was built around a commercial, miniature, multi-contact selector switch that occupied the very center of the product. However, we were given the latitude to propose an alternate design if we desired, but only if the proposal was parallel with a quote that would be based on the design presented to us.

The practice of the military (for as many years as I'd been in the business) was first request bids on a development project for a device that would meet the needs specified by the Procurement Officer. I'd never before seen or heard of an instance where the Procurement Officer had actually attempted to design the thing personally. At any rate, I won't burden the reader with the number and magnitude of the flaws in the officer's design, but it was obvious that his ambition vastly exceeded his capability. I began at once to develop a concept of my own. As required by the RFQ, we submitted the officer's component drawings to our usual range of machine shops to obtain bids on producing a run of 3,000 pieces of each part. We sent the drawings to five different shops for competitive bidding, but only one came back quickly with, "No Bid." When enough time had passed, and the others had not responded, I called one of our favorite shops to ask about the delay getting his quotes back to us.

His response was instructive, "Sorry, I couldn't see the drawings through the tears." It soon became obvious that none of the shops would bid the parts, since it was clear that the officer had no idea how parts like these would normally be machined.

In effect, most of his designs were based on the sort of geometries one would find in components designed for very large production runs (typically found in vacuum cleaners, electric shavers, Etc). Such high production parts would normally be produced by die-casting, for example, or from similar tools that would cost tens of thousands of dollars to create each individual part. In short, it would probably cost $1 million in tooling before the first parts would be struck off. Parts designed (or shaped) for producing by die-casting are nearly impossible to fabricate by manual machining practices. Parts for a run of assemblies as small as 3,000 can only be produced by hand machining, or more likely by computer-programmed machining (from CNC machines). The surface geometries are completely different for high production parts, as compared to short-run processes of manufacture. This switch assembly was short-run.

My quotation problem remained. We wouldn't be able to bid on our own design, without also bidding on the design supplied to us. Finally, to get around the dilemma, I was able to secure machine shop bids, but only if I promised faithfully that we'd never actually order the parts.

As far as our competitors were concerned regarding this RFQ, we knew all of them were effectively out of the running, since the plug and receptacle (at opposite ends of this switch assembly) were proprietary to Thor, and we were the only supplier with the tooling and fixtures needed to make them. Finally as requested, we simultaneously submitted our bids for both the original design, and my own approach, but without revealing the details of the concept I was planning to use. As expected, there was no competition and they looked on our submission with great favor. However, the Naval Air Warfare wanted to know more about my design, and in particular why my approach would cost them one third less than the other design presented.

We arranged a presentation at the Thor plant in Salinas that would outline how my design would be configured to the procurement staff from Naval Air Warfare. If I recall correctly, even Steve didn't know exactly what I had in mind. So as the meeting shifted into high gear, I think he squirmed a bit when I suggested to the customer that I planned an in-house design, not only for the general structure of the device, but also for the actual internal selector switch at the core of the device. The representatives from Naval Air immediately expressed concern at this proposal, since they had already consulted two commercial switch manufacturers for custom designs, and had been quoted six months of development time, at a cost of $250,000 – just for the switch element alone.

As I presented the overall design approach, their concerns mellowed considerably, particularly when we quoted an approximate prototype cost under $100,000 for the entire product, as well as a first article delivery in 10 weeks – core selector switch and all. We got the contract pending final project analysis, and our formal production price quotation. I must add that for the first few weeks, Steve's ulcers did not fair well. The fact was that this entire project could not have been better suited to my nature. It was a perfect example where I could carry a product development effort from initial concept through to its final production, without any obstacles.

One of my better experiences during this project occurred when (based on the manufacturing operations which I'd specified) Steve, in concert with his estimator, determined that each unit would require 11 man-hours of labor time to assemble. However, I conducted my own analysis, by means of actual assembly, rather than intellectual speculation. Once all of the prototype components became available and the specialized assembly and fabrication fixtures (which I'd designed for the project) were completed, I sat down with the company quality control manager and we physically assembled the very first unit. This exercise gave abundant proof that each unit would actually take no more than five and a half man-hours to build. When I presented our findings to Steve, I also encouraged him to actually quote Naval Air-Warfare Center with a final, per unit, production price based on his "standard" estimated time of 11 man-hours – which, in fact, he did. In the months that followed our formal receipt of the production contract, the assembly facilities at Thor (custom fabricated in accordance with my own work-station layouts) successfully manufactured 3,000 units. Our regular staff, who did their jobs at these custom workstations, completed the production run with such efficiency that the project turned out to be the most profitable contracts in the history of Thor. It had been so profitable, in fact, that I received a $20,000 bonus for my successful design and management of the project.

Something from the Heart

As kind, generous and unexpected as the bonus was, it was typical of the many acts of kindness that I experienced during my years at Thor. There was one particularly memorable circumstance where I'd been experiencing a progressively worsening sense of what I thought to be gastritis (or more accurately acid reflux) a condition that seemed to occur with any physical exertion, especially in cold weather. Finally, the symptoms became so uncomfortable and persistent that I made an appointment to see my doctor. As expected, he ran me through a battery of tests, including an EKG.

As he reviewed the seemingly endless printouts that spewed from the machine, I remember thinking "the doctor must have something wrong with his teeth," because every time he paused to look at a particular detail on the EKG printout, he would make a kind of sucking sound with this teeth and shake his head.

Finally, he looked up and said, "Sorry Ron, you don't have gastritis. First thing in the morning you're going to the hospital for an angioplasty. There's a couple of arteries in your heart that look like a kitchen drain after a Thanksgiving dinner!"

I was 60 years old at the time and really hadn't lived a very healthy lifestyle. Among other things, I didn't get enough exercise and my favorite foods were overloaded with fat and cholesterol. Within 48 hours, I was lying on an operating table, and a team of doctors was shoving a tube up the artery in my groin. In the process, they armed a couple of my arteries with stents (which I guess now qualifies me as "bionic"). At any rate, I was released from the hospital five days later and presented with a bill for $27,000.

I recalled thinking at the time, "For a bunch less than that, I could've had a great month on the Riviera, and the food would have been a helluva lot better." Fortunately, Thor had an excellent healthcare plan, which covered my medical expenses, up to a stop-loss of $2,700. In an act of generosity that I will never forget, the Abrams brothers handed me a check that covered the full stop-loss amount. I wasn't surprised; I was astonished!

To this day, I've not had the slightest recurrence of heart problems. As you might expect, that experience was a real wake-up call. During the first year after my surgery, I took up rigorous jogging for at least an hour a day. More importantly, I started to pay serious attention to the nutritional labels on food boxes, packages, cans, and frozen foods, something I still do today.

Once More Into the Breach

The dust of Thor's near bankruptcy had fairly well settled by 1990, and without the demanding burden of development projects for IBM, my workload had significantly scaled back. As a result, I found myself with more free time than ever while working at Thor. With complete access to my personal shop facilities, as well as the factory machine shop 24/7, I encouraged myself to spend many of my leisure hours model building. Soon my old passion for slot machines began to re-assert itself. After a bit of random tinkering, I finally schemed together a concept for a pseudo-antique machine with a design that would focus on a low-cost fabrication approach. The idea was to create a product with runs of a 100 machines or so that could actually be built for about $250 per unit. I really believed that a very low-cost machine, priced between $500-$600, which possessed the nostalgically evocative appearance of a 1920s product, would be very marketable – for people with game rooms or simply to have around the house for general amusement. My research had shown that there were actually many places around the country where private ownership of a slot machine, and particularly one that obviously was not intended for serious casino operation, was perfectly legal. To satisfy the intricate detail that was characteristic of a nostalgic design, rotational molding would prove to be the most practical approach to cabinet construction. Cost containment would be further assisted by a simple, single-pay line logic circuit, and the most incredibly simple reels mechanism I'd ever conceived. To cap off the nostalgia aspect of the idea, the machine was designed to contain a payout unit of minimum complexity, together with a trap-door style, hand-fillable, quick-drop jackpot box that possessed the appearance and operational effect of the original machines. Finally, the residential application of the product eliminated any of the usual security concerns, which would normally have plagued the design of a professional gaming machine, and compounded its cost.

It took a few months of spare time to put a representative prototype together, along with a detailed rendering of what the proposed product would actually look like. When these teaser items were ready, I capped off my efforts by developing a project cost proposal. As soon as I was ready, I casually approached the Abrams brothers with the idea. I'll simply say that they initially seemed less than effervescent in their response to my plans. So it was actually something of a surprise when Steve stopped me in the corridor one day to say that he had been in contact with a coin machine distributor in London and the gentleman had agreed to exhibit our new slot machine at his booth at the Amusement Coin Equipment Show in January. This particular show actually exhibited every year at Alexandra Palace in London. As Steve casually sauntered away, I think I almost lost my upper set. I couldn't believe my ears! It seemed once more that the game was actually afoot!

This little excursion turned out to be the best of all my European travels. We were booked into a great hotel that offered excellent service and meals. What's more, the trip proved totally surprising from the start when I found that Steve had arranged for a tour bus on our first morning. The next day, we met with the distributor and had our first encounter with the spectacle of the Equipment Show. Alexandra Palace was a huge facility built in red brick and iron-lace, with a ceiling that towered three stories above the exhibit floor. Massive radiant heaters located high above offered a modest amount of heating – actually too modest for January. To this day I'm convinced that the people who named Alexandra Palace had apparently been looking in a different direction at the time. All-in-all it was quite exciting – not only to have our own product on public offering, but to see the incredible range of amusement and gaming products that were then on display.

During our visit to the show, we spent several hours making introductions to a range of prospective buyers and other exhibitors. After that day, Steve only allowed us about an hour on the floor of the show before we were off to visit some place of interest. Windsor Palace (a truly magnificent palace indeed) was first on the list. On other days, it was the Tower of London, the War Museum, or Westminster Abbey. In fact, every day was another place of interest that Steve insisted that we see. Every evening began at one fine restaurant or another – all of them excellent– and not a seafood place in the lot. After dinner, it was legitimate theater. There were musicals, comedy shows and allegories, and on one occasion, we actually enjoyed a live performance of *Breaking the Code* with Derek Jacob himself on stage. For those who aren't familiar with this title, the story tells the thrilling and tragic life experience of Alan Turing, the brilliant and socially unconventional genius who was Britain's most accomplished code breaker during World War II. Readers might also recall Derek Jacob in the title role of the massive BBC television production of *I, Claudius*.

The whole trip was a whirlwind delight, but we never sold a single machine. Once more, as we headed for home, I had the distinct sense that this was essentially a repeat of my earlier European travels – travels that were the product of the gracious and generous nature of Nolan Bushnell.

An Inventor by Habit

There was yet one other occurrence during my time at Thor that stands out in my memory – with mixed emotions. During my earliest days at Thor, when I was building the casino-style slot machine, I hired a young draftsman technician aid by the name of yet another Steve – Steve Harrison, who over time became more-or-less my "second in command." Enthusiasm, boundless energy, a sharp intellect, and an endless thirst for skill and knowledge were among his better qualities. Much of what I'd been able to accomplish in my early years at Thor had been supported significantly through Steve's many talents.

Therefore, it was no surprise to me when he announced one day that he was taking a formal course in the machinist's craft. He would bring in examples of the training projects that he'd been required to undertake during his hands-on studies. During one particular casual conversation across his office desk, he showed me the latest of these projects that he'd just completed.

Within seconds, as I fondled the object, I excitedly asked him in astonishment, "Do you realize what you've got here?"

The object was a one-inch diameter steel rod, about ten-inches long. It had been machined with more-or-less conventional but heavy machine screw threads at both ends, and each of these threaded areas was mounted with a large machine-screw nut. It was superficially an unremarkable device, with a design that was simply intended as an exercise in the art of metal machining. The feature that instantly caught my attention was that the two threads were different pitches. That is to say, the two threads (on the metal rod and on each correspond nut) exhibited a slightly different number of threads per inch!

At first young Steve couldn't understand what I was so excited about – until I demonstrated how this unusual combination of features could be used to perform some very remarkable functions. These extraordinary capabilities were the result of the two screw threads pitched at a different number of threads per inch, and the length of a single thread in each of the two features was different by only a few thousands of an inch. If the two nuts were held, in such a way that they could not rotate in relation to each other, then the action of turning the rod within the two nuts would cause these nuts to move in either direction, depending upon which way the rod was rotated. To put it more precisely: if the length of a single thread of one of the thread-features differed from the length of a single thread in the other thread-feature, then a single complete turn of the rod within the related nuts would cause the distance between those nuts to shift by exactly the difference between the two single-thread lengths. That is – if the difference between the two thread dimensions were only 1/1000th of an inch, then each turn of the rod (within the nuts), would cause the distance between those nuts to shift, by only 1/1000th of an inch. In effect, the device would exhibit the performance of a machine-screw thread of 1,000 threads per inch!

No such thread pitch existed in the conventional world of machining. Even if it did exist, the depth of each thread would be so trivial as to effectively give it no strength at all. Since Steve's mechanism yielded the effect of a 1,000 threads per inch, (as a result of two sets of very heavy but similar threads), the net mechanical strength of this device was massive. In other words, one very reasonable application of this new system might be a machine called a screw-jack, the sort of device one uses to jack up one end of a car by the simple turning of a handle with only modest force. The difference here is that one might build a screw-jack with the same kind of handle and the same applied force, but it would have sufficient leverage to lift one end of a locomotive! Of course it would take a thousand turns to lift that end a distance

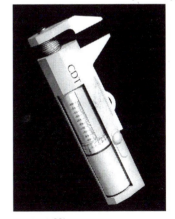

0.0001 Micrometer

of only one inch, but a really trivial electric motor could handle such a job quite easily.

My mind continued to spin with possibilities. Yet another application that came to mind was a potentially vast improvement in the design of a conventional micrometer. For the benefit of those who might not be familiar with this instrument, it's a measuring device to directly read dimensions of small parts, to an accuracy of 1/1000th of an inch, and to interpret such measurements down to 1/10,000th of an inch. The "compound thread" mechanism of Steve's project would also make possible the construction of a micrometer that would directly measure to an accuracy of 1/10,000th of an inch, and to conveniently interpret such a measurement, to readings of 1/100,000th of an inch.

I envisioned these two applications of the mechanism directly and immediately, and within a day or so, many more potential uses came to mind. It seemed to me that this could truly be the first concept of a fundamental mechanism to come to light in the past 100 years. My immediate thought was to proceed with a patent application on the basic concept, in parallel with a patent covering its first practical application, as a direct-reading micrometer. Steve supported and financed the project at once, and within a matter of weeks, formal applications were in the hands of a patent attorney – an attorney I'd previously employed over several years who represented me in the successful issuance of at least six of my earlier patents.

It was an anxious three weeks, as I waited to learn the results of the patent search – a search that would tell me whether any "prior art" of such a device existed within the world of patents. Time dragged on, and when I could tolerate the anxiety any longer, I called the attorney to see if anything had been discovered. On that occasion I apparently caught him "on the fly," so to speak. He was apparently running to catch a plane. To keep things as brief as possible, I simply asked if anything had been learned.

Explaining that he was pressed for time, he simply blurted back, "We've found nothing yet! It all looks good!" At that point, as far as I was concerned, I had that money banked and spent! It really seemed as though I had the world by the tail! After all the years of trying, I'd finally hit the jackpot!

There is an old expression that reads, "Anytime that something looks too good to be true, it usually is." The attorney's formal report (the actual results of the patent search) showed up two weeks later to advise, not only that the basic concept was probably 100 years old, but nearly every possible application for the device had already been patented in the United States, or in other countries around the world.

This was not the first time that my house of cards had come crashing down – nor would it be the last.

Retirement – The First Go Around

It was early 1997, and I was 63 years old. My understanding of the "nature of money" gained through careful inquiry over a span of decades, had encouraged me to build a long-term savings in the form of a healthy cache of gold and silver coins. It was savings based on a belief that any nation's money, that consisted of nothing but worthless paper was guaranteed to steadily shrink in buying power, and inevitably collapse entirely. It was my absolute belief that I could best preserve the buying power of my savings, by saving in a form that actually satisfied that function, for the past 3,000 years – gold and silver coins. At the same time, I'd never actually deprived myself, for the sake of this savings agenda. In fact, to quote a line from John Mortimer (*Rumpole of the Bailey*), I truly believed that "no pleasure on Earth was worth sacrificing, for the sake of five more years in a geriatric ward." The fact is, I'd built up enough of a reserve to allow myself to think seriously of getting some real pleasure out of life before it was too late. However, I also appreciated the part I was playing in the long-term prosperity of the company, not to mention my very real responsibility to the Abrams brothers for the many kindnesses they'd shown me over the years. With these obligations in mind, I informed Steve of my intention to retire, effectively on my 65th birthday – some two years down the road. We all agreed this timeframe was not unreasonable, and it would be an adequate amount of time to find someone to properly replace me.

Time seems to pass more quickly as one grows older. But even so, those two years seemed to whiz by, and in 1999, I finally took my leave from Thor. I'd been paying into the Social Security pool for well over 30 years – although I never actually expected to ever see a dime of it again. But astonishing as it was, having waited to the age of 65, I found myself in the comfortable position of drawing the maximum monthly stipend, and hopefully would continue to do so for the rest of my life. As part of my regular remuneration over the many years of my employment, Steve had always provided me with a company car. Now upon my retirement, he presented me with the Chevy Lumina that had been bought new only two years earlier. In fact, he even offered to buy me a brand new car upon my departure. But I insisted that such generosity would be neither necessary, nor appropriate.

*****

At the time of my retirement, Harmon had long since finished a 20-year stint with the Marine Corps and was living with his family in a home he'd bought in El Cajon, California in the 1960s. He was not only drawing his Marine Corps retirement and his Social Security, but had also established a modest import business that had served him well for more than a decade. Between these incomes, he managed to enter the beginnings of a comfortable and well-earned old age. Years earlier, Harmon and I had come to an understanding concerning Mama. Effectively since he had a family to support and I did not, we agreed that I would take full responsibility for seeing that Mama was properly provided for as she grew older. Since the time we'd bought our first house so many decades before, I had kept up with all of the mortgage payments on that house, as well as on the subsequent homes that we'd owned in the years that followed, now all of them in my own name.

It was during the late 1970s, however, that one final nasty encounter with California's "unequal" Board of Equalization (a property tax agency) led to a drastic change in my residency. I won't burden the reader with the complicated details, other than to say that by exercising an obscure subtlety in the property tax laws, the agency suddenly notified me of their intention to double my property taxes. They intended to utilize a legal device that would circumvent the Prop 13 limitation – a limitation that was supposed to prevent the state from increasing the tax on any residential property by more than 5% per year.

When I tried to resolve the issue through a phone conversation with the tax agent, I finally became so furious at his arrogance that I told him flat out, "What you're trying to do to me in this matter can legally be done in California, only between properly married couples, and you can do it to someone else. Not me!"

Unfortunately, I was simply too involved in my office work to undertake a demanding effort to sell one house and buy another. So instead I'd told Mama to immediately put the house up for sale and to find a nice alternative residence in Tucson to replace it. Her extensive business experience over the years gave me confidence that she would be able to deal effectively with such an undertaking. I chose Tucson because I had come to enjoy both the climate and the casual character of the town during my first two years of employment at Thor.

The California house was originally purchased several years earlier for $57,000, but over the years I'd made a number of improvements to the property. One of these improvements was a somewhat whimsical remodeling of the living room. The shape of this room was actually quite unusual to start with, rectangular with windows centered in one of the long walls. Best of all, it had a pitched ceiling with a central beam at its peak that ran the length of the room. I think it was my sense of the dramatic that led me to envision an artful, Victorian style in this room. It seemed to me that this could be readily accomplished if I simply employed my skills as a model builder and detailed the room like a model, but life-sized. I began by fabricating a three-foot high mahogany wainscoting in panels of uniform width around all the walls. Then I sectionally framed the upper walls in thin dark-wood molding. These framed panels of the upper walls were filled in with maroon and gold, foliated and flocked wallpaper. It was modestly embarrassing when I'd selected this particular wallpaper, and the salesman wanted to know if I was going to open a bordello. Hanging, sconce-like, Victorian lamps were projected out from the end walls. The peaked ceiling construction yielded triangular sections at the top of both end walls, like the pediments of a building, and formed perfect sites for incidental paintings. I framed these areas with thin dark-wood molding, and these enclosed triangular spaces with sylvan scenes in faded pastel tones, so typical of late Victorian styling. One scene was done in a Grecian theme, while on the opposite end wall, the styling was Roman. The final effect was exactly what I'd hoped for: dramatic and bold.

To this day, I believe that the successful stylization of this room was responsible for selling the house within four days of listing. It sold easily for $114,000. On her own, Mama picked out a very nice three-bedroom, two bath ranch-style home in the south end of Tucson, just south of the Tohono O'Odham Indian Reservation.

She had formally retired from her working life in the late 1970s, and had begun an early drawing of her Social Security at age 62. This meant that her drawing was substantially reduced, and worse yet remained her entire income. My own earnings, as well as the support of my long-term savings, made certain that there would be no difficulty in assuring her complete security. I was even able to provide her with a new car and a few other comforts. By the time that I retired, Mama had been keeping the Tucson house in good order for more than 20 years.

The early years of my post-Thor retirement were quite comfortable, and the freedom that I was finally enjoying (not having to go to work every morning) allowed me to pursue a wider range of interests than I'd ever known. It was really great – for a year or two – until the sameness began to set in. To follow any interest I might choose was pleasant enough, but over time there just wasn't any challenge left. And even in my late sixties, I still had enough internal drive to feel that there was something missing from my life. Tucson wasn't exactly the Riviera (although it was surrounded by a thousand square miles of beach.) I think that it was my childhood illusion of a "South Seas" environment – as characterized by sandy beaches and swaying palms – that made my fancy turn to the beach communities in Florida. Whatever it was, I started to casually scan real estate when a really fantastic house popped up in the small town of Ormond Beach, located just a few minutes from Daytona Beach. And I couldn't believe the price! After several phone calls and some additional research, I caught a flight to Florida to see the property first hand.

The house was exactly as described. It encompassed 5,500 square feet of floor space plus a three-car garage. There was an upstairs game room that occupied 600 square feet with built-in amenities, and even a regulation pool table that was listed as part of the property. Directly below the game room was a 600 square foot kitchen with an island stove, grill and sink – in addition to a second double-sink against the windowed back wall. Other kitchen built-ins included a six-foot wide refrigerator/freezer. The sliding back doors of the kitchen opened onto the patio, which surrounded a 50- foot free-form swimming pool. More than that, the backyard fence and gate marked the dividing line between the property and the St. Andrews Golf Course. There were six bedrooms plus four full baths. The massive living room even sported one wall that was totally mirrored, floor to ceiling giving the impression of a room-space the size of a ballroom. Total selling price: $220,000.

I signed the paperwork at once, and within three months Mama and I had moved in. One might ask – why would two people need all this space? My answer to that is simple. I took the master bedroom for myself, along with its private bath. I might add that huge bathroom was loaded with amenities I'd never seen before (outside of the movies). The next largest bedroom (next to the kitchen) and private bath was turned over to Mama. By this time she was already spending most of her time getting around the house in her electric wheelchair. Another room, which came complete with floor-to-ceiling bookcases, was turned into my first-ever complete library. The room next to it was outfitted as a fully equipped electronics lab. Of the remaining bedrooms, one served as a guest room, while the runt of the litter provided excellent storage space – a convenience not adequately provided in most houses.

Retirement – Interrupted

One thing that I hadn't properly allowed for, was the costly maintenance of our new home – with the mortgage and all, it was something over $4,000 per month. With nothing but our Social Security checks, I soon began to cut into my long-term savings at an uncomfortable rate. At first I gained some relief by casually dealing in collector's stamps and coins via eBay, but within a year, it was evident that a serious source of real and steady income would be needed soon.

My first attempts at finding work followed the same tried-and-true methods that previously worked with great success. First to come to mind was the Job Shop approach. Unfortunately, Central Florida wasn't the heavily industrialized environment of Southern California. No such shops existed and places like Manpower didn't really cater to my kind of talents. I tried headhunters next. Several were listed in the area, and formal applications were immediately filed. They initially seemed to offer some promise, but again it soon became obvious that I'd never find a descent position via that channel.

Finally, when I'd totally lost patience, and the want ads offered no worthy prospects, I grabbed the phonebook and turned to the pages marked

"Engineering Companies." Only three listed seemed to involve my kind of work, or even looked as though they might need my type of skill set. Formal, unsolicited resumes were mailed off to each of the companies. Two of them never responded at all. Not a "thank you," or "no thank you," or "not interested," or even, "Drop dead. Go to hell." But the third, a company by the name of Ocean Design, did respond to my inquiry. The chief engineer, a fellow named John Toth, actually invited me in for an interview. It proved to be one of the most interesting interviews I ever had. In a talk that ran nearly an hour, we discussed everything from my 16-year stint as chief engineer at Thor to my involvement in the origins of Apple Computer. I think he was mostly moved by my 50 years in drafting, product design, engineering and product development. Eventually, he suggested a 60-day trial period as a consultant. Then, most apologetically, he asked if I would accept a starting salary at the same rate as when I had left Thor.

In a somewhat fumbling response, I suggested, "That seems quite reasonable." Finally, he advised that "at the moment," he didn't have an office, or even a drawing board available and would I mind working at home? He'll never know how close I came at that moment to leaping across his desk to kiss him on the forehead.

As I was leaving his office, he threw me a last question, "You do work in AutoCAD, of course?" When I said "no," his comeback was, "That's OK. I'm sure you'll pick it up in a couple of weeks."

It was quite a surprise to me, but he was absolutely right. It had never occurred to me before, but the college and trade-school courses in the use of AutoCAD computer drafting – courses that often took six months or more – actually devoted much of that time to teaching students the basic intricacies of drafting – such as title blocks, format, line weights, geometry and the mathematics of the art! My entire career had been spent on the drawing board and my skills at this craft were such that I could lay lead perhaps three times faster than almost anyone I'd ever met. More than that, I knew all the tricks of the craft. So all I really had to learn was how to manipulate all of the principle devices of the electronic drafting program.

Ocean Design was a closed corporation whose owner had created a most remarkable sub-oceanic device many years earlier. It was an electrical cable connector set that could tolerate the conditions on the ocean floor at depths of two miles or more, and could be mated and/or dismated within such incredible depths of seawater. To those who might not be aware, the sea floor is one of the most abusive environments on Earth, particularly at depths of a mile or more. Sand and silt are a constant threat to any kind of mechanism, not to mention an unimaginable range of animal, fish and vegetable life. It is an environment where pressures are scaled in the thousands of pounds per square inch – unlike our surface-bound environment where the surrounding pressure is only about 15 pounds per square inch. The initial field of application for this product had been the oil and gas industry, principally for use on offshore oil-drilling platforms.

In addition to his many other responsibilities, John had pressed management to exploit this exceptional technology into more far-reaching fields than simply the oil and gas industry. In fact he'd been sufficiently forceful that he was assigned to lead a new department called DOT (Defense, Oceanographic and Telecommunications). His efforts at marketing in these fields had been so successful that he needed a "Second in Command" to assist in innovative product development. That's where I came in. When I started at Ocean Design, I might be called into a meeting between John and a prospective client – a client with some unusual technical application where no standard oceanographic equipment or device was currently available. On several occasions, I witnessed the customer outlining the nature of his problem to John, often with drawings or some other kind of documents that collectively made up a "request for quote."

John would then review the documentation (with nodding approval), and then unexpectedly hand it to me with the comment, "Here Wayne. See what you can do with this."

The meeting would end with my boss telling the client, "No problem. We'll have a quote for ya in a couple of days." Then John would take off on a totally different track, confident that I'd be back to him within a reasonable amount of time with a workable design and a cost analysis.

One of the most interesting and most demanding projects came from Northrop Grumman. We had no idea of the intended application, or purpose, but apparently the company was involved in some sort of sub-oceanic work, and had acquired an ROV (Remote Operated Vehicle). An ROV is a small, un-manned sub-sea vehicle that is linked to an operator on a maintenance ship or similar vessel via a controlling electrical cable. This Remote Operated Vehicle is usually equipped with lights, video cameras, and with some sort of grappling and/ or manipulating arm/s, all designed to perform submerged maintenance, control, salvage or other functions. In this case, Northrop Grumman's particular application apparently involved the manual mating

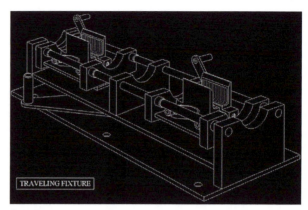

TRAVELING FIXTURE

Sub-sea connector "mating-rig" that Ron designed and built for Northrop Grumman while at Ocean Design

and dismating of sub-sea connectors. For some reason that we were never able to discover, the ROV they'd acquired (at very great expense) only had a single manipulating arm. Aside from the fact that the typical sub-sea connector set is six-to-eight inches in diameter, up to two feet long and weighs up to 50 pounds or more, it also requires 50 to 75 pounds of force to mate, and/or dismate. None of these characteristics were beyond the capability of a typical ROV manipulator. The real problem was that a connector set consisted of two parts – a plug and a receptacle, and this particular ROV had only one arm!

To solve this obvious problem, the client had previously approached another engineering company and spent nearly $100,000 in an effort to create a mechanism that would enable their one-arm ROV to manipulate a typical two-part connector set. After months of trying, the resultant device – with its hydraulic controls and electronic regulating systems (and who knows what else) never worked properly. Finally, in desperation, Northrop came to Ocean Design since we were the company that had manufactured the connector set they were using. After a careful review of the task, I decided on a relatively simple, and totally mechanical solution. My new design involved the use of a heavy base-plate fitted with two parallel guide rods that ran the full length of the plate. Mounted on these guide rods, I provided two carriages that moved towards or away from each other by the simple turning of a crank that extended from the side of the device. This crank, which operated through the substantial leverage realized by a worm-and-spur drive, was able to move the carriages in either direction with very substantial force, depending on which way the crank was rotated. In addition, each carriage was designed so that when the two carriages were farthest apart, a plug of one cable-end could be dropped onto it, and when pressed into place, a self-locking clamp would fix that plug into a precisely fixed position. Then the receptacle of the other cable-end would similarly be secured to the remaining carriage. Then it was only a matter of rotating the crank in order to bring the carriages together with enough force to easily mate the connector set. To reverse the process, it was only necessary to be sure that the carriages were fully brought together, and to position and lock the mated connector set into place. Rotating the crank handle in the opposite direction provided all the force needed for the set to easily separate. Release levers enabled the separated connector set to be freed from the mating/dismating machine.

I wasn't quite comfortable with the idea of simply offering sketches and concept drawings to the client to convey the nature of the device that I was proposing. So for the presentation, I decided to unleash my passion for model building. I quickly fabricated a fully functional, one-quarter scale miniature of the complete mechanism, and the connector set that it would control. The meeting came off perfectly. So much so, that when I demonstrated the workings of the device, it seemed as if the clients viewed the presentation as if it was something good to eat. They were enthralled! When we quoted a final prototype price of $58,000, there was no doubt in the mind of my boss, or anyone else that the sale was clinched. Within the week, the deal was finalized.

Things started to move quickly after the project was green lit. It took about 10 days to create a complete set of component fabrication drawings, and hand over the entire document package to the Ocean Design Purchasing Department. After that, another seven weeks would pass before all of the purchased and fabricated parts would arrive at the company's dock. That's when I received the most unusual call from John, who informed me the Receiving Department and Quality Control had no personnel available. He most apologetically asked me if I'd please come down to the plant and personally perform the inspection – essentially to verify the dimensional accuracies of each of the parts.

I remember telling John at that point, "Inspection is not my usual function, but at these rates, I'd do windows." Once I was satisfied as to the overall quality of the vendor-supplied parts, I was then told that no technician shop time was available either, and would I mind taking on the task of putting the machine together myself? It took me two days before I had the unit fully assembled to a point where it would be ready for demonstration, first to John and then to the client. Both demonstrations were profoundly successful.

Up until now, I'd thought that the most perfect job I ever worked was the 16 years I had spent with Thor. The working relationship that had formed between John and I over the last few months went far beyond anything I might have otherwise dreamed. I enjoyed the comfort of working at home at my own schedule. I came and went as I pleased and the projects I was involved with were totally fascinating. More importantly, instead of diminishing my long-term savings, I was regularly adding to its total with a steady paycheck.

My enjoyment of the job reached a high point one day during a casual conversation with my boss. We were discussing the general qualities and merits of oceanic "wet-mateable" connectors, when John happened to float a random comment, citing the one major problem that still existed in that field – namely, the inability to mate or dismate these connector sets while the cable was still electrically energized. So the reader understands the issue: when these connectors are used on cables intended for trans-oceanic communication, the lines can run many thousands of miles long. The accumulated electrical resistance, even using copper wire in cables of such a great length, made the communication of signals almost impossible without amplification. In fact the only way to resolve the problem was to install amplifying repeater stations at several-hundred mile intervals along the line. These fully automated and environmentally sealed stations, in turn, needed power in order to operate. But to transmit the level of power needed for these stations across great distances required a very high voltage, usually in the order of 10,000 volts, at one end of the cable. This meant the insulated wire would carry a voltage that was so potent that one didn't have to grab such a wire to risk injury – since that level of voltage could readily "arc out" to get you. In short when a cable fitted with mated connectors was fully energized, the act of separating such a connector set would yield a massive (even explosive) electrical arc that was powerful enough to completely destroy the face of the connector. As destructive as such an accident might be if it occurred in the air, one can imagine the effect if it happened while immersed in saltwater on the ocean floor. John's comment simply related to the fact that while a wet-mateable connector solved many problems with sub-oceanic technology, what the industry really needed was a connector that would be "hot-mateable" as well. The actual difficulties involved in building a "hot-mate" connector set are easier to appreciate when one understands the physics of "very long high-voltage" cables.

It is simpler to appreciate this problem once you understand the simple construction of a fundamental electrical component called a "capacitor." A capacitor in its simplest form is made of two metal plates that are separated by insulating non-conducting material. If a voltage is applied to these plates (across the insulating material) and then removed, an electric charge is physically stored within the device (like a battery) between the plates. The charge can then be relieved by providing an electrically conductive path that would join the two plates together, completing a circuit. Moreover, the magnitude of the charge stored is dependent upon the surface area of the two metal plates. This last factor (the area of the plates), relates directly to the problem we're discussing. The larger the surface area of the plates of any capacitor, the more massive the stored charge.

Now consider this factor, in relation to an electrical cable that is thousands of miles long! If we now recognize that the inner conductor of the cable is essentially one "plate" of our capacitor, and the metallic cable shield (outer metal jacket) is the second "plate," and the non-conducting jacket of the inner conductor is the "insulator," it becomes obvious that such a cable is now an unbelievably massive capacitor! When we apply 10,000 volts to the cable, we will instantly charge that capacitor to an incredible extent, perhaps 100,000 watts of potential power. Under such circumstances, how is it possible to separate the connector set without catastrophic consequences? To turn off the power source would accomplish nothing, in terms of the massive charge still held within the cable itself. In today's world, the way this problem is solved (after the power source is turned off) is to employ a very sophisticated means to "bleed off" the huge charge that is still stored within a multi-thousand mile long cable. This action must be performed before the connector set

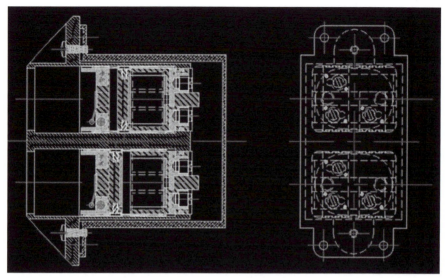

"NEMA-12 explosion-proof" 15R outlet prototype that Ron designed for Ocean Design

can safely be separated. This is a very tedious, technically demanding and time-consuming procedure.

Yet even with that understanding in mind, at the instant of John's comment, a miraculous flash of instinct struck me as I blurted out to him, "No problem. I can do that!"

That was the first and only time I ever saw John do a double-take. After several quick comments, he finally came back with, "That's something you're going to have to show me!" His jaw seemed to visibly drop, as I sketched out the method I would use.

It seemed so incredibly simple to me that I couldn't understand why no one had done it before. My sketch described the use of a high-voltage switch within the body of the connector, a switch that would separate the cable (with its massive charge) from the contacts in the face of the connector. This internal switch was designed to open (electrically separate) as soon as any attempt was made to disengage the connector set. The action automatically interrupted and insulated all of the connector contacts in the face of the connector, at the precise moment that a separation of the connector set was attempted.

This internal switching mechanism would be operated magnetically, so that no mechanical (physical) linkage to the switch would be needed.

Finally, the switch mechanism would be sealed within a vacuum-filled cavity, with sufficient contact spacing so that no electrical arcing could occur when the circuits were opened. When re-mating the connector set, all of the connector contacts (the plug and receptacle) would be made to fully engage, before the internal switch would close again. Using this method, the exposed contacts at the face of the receptacle would be electrically "dead," before the connector set could be separated, even though the very long cable would remain fully charged.

John was sufficiently impressed with the idea that he immediately gave me leave to build a functioning prototype of the magnetically-actuated internal, high-voltage switch. The demonstration mechanism was completed in a week's time, and was taken to the lab for testing, where it demonstrated successful performance at a potential in excess of 10,000 volts. Once more in my life, I had every reason to believe that I'd finally hit the jackpot!

The time that I'd spent building the demonstration switch, of course, had been fully paid for by Ocean Design, since I was under salary. Likewise the cost of the laboratory testing, with the aid of the Lab Manager, had also been covered on Ocean Design's dime. What the reader must now understand is that the conventional practice with all engineering personnel, under the terms of their employment, is that anything that one might invent during one's tenure, even if the invention has nothing in common with the employer's business activities, is legally the property of the employer. Nonetheless, I fully expected at this point that management would allow John and I to proceed at once to develop the first practical hot-mate connector to be marketed within the wet-mate oceanic-connector industry. With that effort successfully completed I felt certain that the company, and eventually myself, would both realize a fortune. In fact, I went on feeling certain of that inevitable result for the many weeks that followed – and even for the many months that followed that – as the concept and its potential remained endlessly dormant. Ocean Design top management did absolutely nothing.

*****

169

After nearly two years, without the slightest effort made by the front office to pursue the development of this concept, I totally lost patience with them, and began to consider other applications for this idea. I pressed John to approach management with a request, that if they didn't want to use my invention, to formally release the thing to me, so that I might exploit it in other possible applications. Naturally, when John asked what exactly was the application I was considering, I told him, "A NEMA-12, 15R outlet."

The idea that had come to my mind was an ordinary household electrical outlet that would conform to the NEMA-12 standard. NEMA is the acronym for the National Electrical Manufacturer's Association, and the "-12" standard is referred to as "explosion-proof." That doesn't mean that products under this standard would withstand an explosion, but that such products will not "initiate" an explosion. Environments such as coalmines and grain elevators contain atmospheres (gases, dust particles, whatever) that are excessively prone to explosion, needing only a spark (electrical or otherwise) to trigger devastating consequences. Any piece of electrical equipment that is plugged into any standard electrical outlet that might be unplugged from that outlet while it was still turned on will inherently yield an electric spark, between the contacts of that outlet and the plug contacts. Common electrical duplex outlets, such as are used in any home or business, are physically specified under the NEMA designation "15R."

My plan was simply to design a duplex, NEMA 15R outlet that could be directly interchangeable with any standard wall outlet, but would be built around my hot-mate concept. Such an outlet would be intended for use not only in mines, but could be used in grain elevators, ether-filled hospital operating rooms, and in places like auto repair shops with risk-prone atmospheres that might (at various times) be filled with gasoline fumes or other explosive vapors.

Beyond the design of the outlet itself, I had also conceived an overall plan for its effective exploitation, starting with a patent application that would cover not only the product itself, but also the fundamental concept. We would then proceed, as I'd envisioned the plan, with fabrication of a prototype to be subjected to the complete range of NEMA qualification tests, but in our own labs. After a patent search had confirmed the virtual certainty of a successful issuance of a formal patent, a short production run would be made to yield several hundred copies of the product to then be formally submitted to NEMA and to any other government and/or industrial qualification agencies, for universal approval. The successful conclusion of all of these activities would then be followed by applications to all the major regulatory agencies involved with the writing and issuance of building codes – agencies who might then specify this "type" of product for use in any environment/s that might experience explosive atmospheres.

I further suggested, as part of my proposal, that it would be foolish, even after having successfully completed all of the foregoing preparatory actions, to even think of actually going into the business of manufacturing and marketing our newly qualified product. Instead it would seem far wiser, at that stage, to simply take out a full-page ad in each of the several industrial

Ethel (mother) and Pat (sister-in-law), 1980s

magazines that serve that industry – an ad that would invite bids from Eagle, Leviton, GE, or any other current manufacturers of this type of product, for the exclusive rights to manufacture and market this "newly qualified" electrical outlet. In short, I proposed that we would solicit the entire range of these manufacturers to discover who would like to own this industry.

John was sufficiently intrigued by my proposal that he immediately granted me leave to build the design phase of the project and to prepare the necessary documentation for a formal patent search. It was a few weeks later, when my designs for the prototype stage of development were virtually complete, that I pressed to learn whether or not our patent search had exposed any prior art. At first all the reports came back, indicating that we had a clear field – until one morning when I came into the office, only to be handed a copy of someone else's issued patent – a patent that was then only two weeks old! My warnings to John, when I'd first expressed the idea to him, had not been heeded. If they had been, that patent would then have been in the name of Ronald G. Wayne, assigned to Ocean Design. Instead, once more in my life, I was a day late and a dollar short. It was then that I determined that "enough was enough." I would never again invest so much as another ounce of effort into this kind of exercise in futility.

Unfortunately by then, an atmosphere had been building for some time, which foretold the end of my employment with ODI. I'd finally come to understand something about the politics of departmental management at Ocean Design, and what had actually been going on in the upper echelons of the company. As I'd finally come to learn, there was an underlying reason for why no tech-time, or inspection, or QA hours had been available for the Northrop-Grumman project – and why we had to order the machine parts for that product from outside shops, despite the fact that Ocean Design housed massive machine shop facilities of their own. It also became evident as to why no in-house office space was available for my use. All of these circumstances had been part of a pattern of behavior on the part of upper management, (from my point of view) to apparently restrict the capabilities of the DOT department, with whose operating premise they fundamentally disagreed. I will never know the exact details of the conflicts that surrounded the strained relationship between the DOT department, and upper management of Ocean Design, but that troublesome strain seemed to adversely affect every aspect of our working environment.

Finally, having tolerated this strain to the limits of his patience, John offered his resignation, and the department was turned over to other hands. The person who took up the reigns of DOT was a most pleasant, amiable and competent engineer. But unfortunately, I believe that he lacked John's rare quality of focused energy, and skilled judgment – qualities that had been the principle force which had enabled the department to achieve its previous successes. And so, (as I understood it) when the previous levels of profits began to decline after John's departure, the company management felt that they could do without my services as well. While I hadn't been anxious to leave, I also noted that much of the fire, the spark, the exhilaration of my job under John's leadership, had faded, and as we all learn from life, all good things must inevitably come to an end.

*****

After moving to Florida some years earlier, the deteriorating aspects of Mama's advancing age had begun to show in many subtle, but telling ways. She had settled into the comfort of using her electric wheelchair to such an extent that she began to seriously lose her ability to walk without significant discomfort. Then there was a progressive decline in the state of her mental faculties – so much so that it finally became necessary to relocate her to an assisted living facility where she could receive proper attention around the clock. Florida, being a geriatric state, had many such institutions around the Daytona Beach area. The place I selected turned out to be located only a few miles from the house, which made it easy for me to visit her several times each week. During each of these visits, I would always bring along a treat of some kind, mostly in the form of a lox and cream-cheese sandwich. She had a passion for these throughout her life. The facility was highly skilled at comfortably dealing with the effects of her advancing years. But, of course, they could do nothing to significantly mitigate the iron teeth of time. Within six months of her admission to the home, she quietly passed away at age 92.

Effectively, I was then left alone in the great house. Moreover, the best job I ever had in my life was also gone. The aura of my living environment had noticeably darkened and I sensed that it was time for me to move on once more. This time, I sought more practical living accommodations and an opportunity to relieve the depression that circumstances had imposed on me. I soon drifted back to the computer to scan the housing market for something that would be better suited to my newly revised circumstances. The immediate focus was to find a place with no state income tax. This narrowed the field substantially. Only Florida or Nevada seemed to fit this requirement, and to be honest, for some reason that escapes me at the moment, I was psychologically bent to the Nevada side of the equation. In a relatively short amount of time, I found what seemed to be the ideal offering. Some places around Las Vegas looked tempting, but my natural aversion to crowds and heavy traffic in particular quickly crossed that city off my list of considerations. I soon found an intriguing property in the small town of Pahrump, Nevada. Pahrump was a small town that straddled State Highway

160, at about 60 miles due west of Las Vegas, not far from the California border. I immediately arranged for a quick flight out to McCarren International in Las Vegas, where a rental car got me to the site within an hour and a half. I had only to walk in the front door to recognize that this was the place. The lot, in the middle of an overgrown desert, was a full 1-1/4 acres. It sported a 1,200-square-foot, pre-manufactured house positioned about 50 feet back from the quiet, residential street. There was another 900-square-foot pre-manufactured building another 50 feet back from the front house. Curiously enough, this back house was not considered part of the actual real estate, but instead was regarded as personal property, which required a separate tax payment to Nye County. Each house was four-bedrooms, two-baths, and neither house was more than eight years old. I immediately adopted the front house to be the main residence, with the back house reserved for shop, lab and storage facilities.

There weren't any streetlights or curbing along the residential streets in Pahrump, with the exception of several small, fenced and gated housing developments. But at the same time, the houses were sufficiently scattered to avoid any sense of crowding. The town of Pahrump boasted a population of some 40,000 residents, but this population was scattered over a township of 400 square miles. I found it fascinating that while I was signing the papers in the realtor's office two calls came in expressing interest in the property I'd just bought. Interesting timing!

Once more, it took about three months to fully relocate to my new home, including another five-day, cross-country drive – mostly by way of I-10. The year was 2004, and in the process of making the move to Pahrump, I succeeded in selling the Florida house where I was able to clear roughly $110,000. Of this amount, I laid out about half as down payment on the Pahrump property, which was priced at roughly $150,000. The remaining half was used to buy gold at $400 per ounce. That same gold at this writing is priced at nearly $1,700 per ounce. This acquisition of gold was not simply a lucky shot, but the result of a lifetime's study into the "nature of money," and was simply added to my lifelong savings in metals.

So at 70 years of age, I was settled once again into a tolerably comfortable home. I had a bit of money in the bank and a substantial holding in precious metals – at least enough to insure my long-term security, particularly since I was drawing the maximum Social Security allotment. Since I'd fully outfitted the back house as a shop and lab, I effectively had my own sandbox and all the toys I could play with. But what I didn't have was relief from the effects of living completely alone. The fact is that in a life that consisted of darting from one job to another, from one "will-o'-the-wisp" to another, from one invention scheme to another, I'd long ago settled into a lifestyle where I could follow whatever adventure I desired. That free wheeling habit of living never seemed to allow for any possibility of raising a family. Perhaps, psychologically, I was never willing to take the responsibility, or maybe I never met a woman who could put up with me. Whatever the reason, I was beginning to wonder how I would manage my affairs in my "reclining years" when age would work its effects on me, as it does upon all of us.

I'd been living in the new residence for about a year when I suddenly thought of my friend and former co-worker, Scott Bellairs, and of all the burdens that life had pressed upon him. Here was the one person in the whole wide world who I could honestly say, "I would trust that man with my life." I hadn't had serious contact with the man for a considerable time, aside from a few casual phone conversations. It was not until I got back in touch with him that I'd learned the details of how his life had evolved during the preceding eight or nine years.

I attended his wedding some 25 years earlier, and in the time that followed, his wife, Michelle, bore him three children – two girls and a boy. Unfortunately by the time their son was born, Michelle, who had battled psychological issues, had drifted into a deep state of alcoholism that tragically left their son, Michael, with Fetal Alcohol Syndrome. By shear luck, the only pronounced symptom of the condition was a serious learning deficiency. In all other respects, one couldn't ask for a finer son. He's a handsome young man now, with a completely loving and well-behaved nature. Michelle, however, passed away when Michael was only 12 years old.

It seemed to me that the perfect solution for everyone concerned would be for Scott to bring his family to Pahrump where I would set them up in the back house. For all the years I'd known him, Scott had always been zealously self-sufficient. Until a few years earlier, he'd made his living by operating a residential/business cleaning service, until he was no longer able to work because of the effects of the cleaning chemicals. Even after that, he still managed to care and provide for his family – no matter how

Left to right: Candice Bellairs, Mary Bellairs, Kai Brown, Michael Bellairs, Kathleen Hone Scott Bellairs & Ron Wayne, 2010.

difficult the effort. With the assistance that I would provide for himself and his family, problems of that nature would be a thing of the past. In effect, beyond whatever he could provide for himself, I would undertake to fill whatever gap might arise, essentially for the rest of his life. In return I hadn't the remotest doubt that when the time arrived, Scott would provide the necessary services I would need for the rest of my days.

By the time I'd contacted him with this proposal in mid-2005, Scott had established a common-law relationship with April Travis, who had a son from an earlier marriage. Her boy, Corey, was about three years younger than Michael, but with the older boy's slight mental limitations, the kids established a truly excellent relationship, almost as if they were the same age. They each readily and totally assumed the mantel of brother. At the same time, April had proved to be the most perfect mate that Scott could have hoped for, and together we took on the status of "the perfect family." During the first few years of this arrangement, both Scott and April found good paying jobs – Scott worked as a pizza deliveryman and April worked as the second-tier manager in the kitchens at a local gentlemen's leisure-pleasure facility on the outskirts of Pahrump.

As the years went by, however, both the economic situation and our household economics began to deteriorate. First, with the declining economy, Scott's delivery job went away. Then a short time later, April, for some inexplicable reason, lost her sense of smell, a condition that made working in a culinary position, virtually impossible. Over the next six months, we tried everything to discover the cause of April's problem, until finally a series of medical tests identified her condition: cancer of the frontal sinus. For the next 10 months, every possible treatment was attempted, ending with a three-month's stint at the Mayo Clinic in Phoenix, Arizona. She underwent every imaginable torment of treatment from surgery to chemotherapy, and radiation. The only result was to postpone the inevitable. At 39 years old, April passed away in January of 2010. At her request, Corey remained in the permanent care of Scott.

During the time of April's illness, one other change was made in our family relationship. Scott's mother had lost her house to foreclosure in California at the age of 69. I invited her to essentially take over half of our forward house immediately as her new and permanent home. After April's passing, all of us settled into a most amicable family group. After years of living together, Scott, who lost his biological father at a very early age, has comfortably accustomed himself to the habit of calling me "Dad," and I've thoroughly enjoyed the title and status of "Grampa" in the eyes of the boys. Shortly after Scott and his family relocated to Pahrump, both of his daughters went off to start families of their own.

An Old Friend Returns

It was mid-2008 when I got a call from my old boss at ODI, John Toth. Even before his time at Ocean Design, John had been a registered professional engineer. So when he left the company, instead of looking for another full-time job, he decided to continue his career as a freelance consulting engineer in the field of oceanographic equipment. According to the terms of his departure from ODI, John was required to refrain from any engineering activity that would compete with the products of his former employer for a period (I believe) of two years. But once he had honored that non-compete commitment, he began to think in terms of a totally new type of wet-mateable connector – a connector that would employ a design that would circumvent many of the inherent limitations of the ODI product. However, John found his activities as a consulting engineer were so successful that he had no time to devote himself to that project. Finally, he learned of my retirement and asked me to assist him in turning his concept into a real product design. Since we had worked so well together over the years, this seemed like a mutually beneficial partnership. Even beyond this, I was also able to aid him in preparing all necessary material for a patent application. We readily agreed on a nominal salary for a project that would last four to five months. In reality, the problems of such a design were so demanding that it was nearly a year and half before we'd reached a point that John was sufficiently content with what had been accomplished. While a completely final design was not achieved, and no physical hardware was ever created, it was still (as a creative exercise) one of my more exciting projects. And yet, there is always the hope that at some time in the future, a real product might come out of our diligent efforts. But as of this writing, the evolution of John's new connector remains an open book.

*****

Aside from the work on John's connector concept, and a few trivial design/drafting jobs that have intermittently come in from Thor, I continue to support my self exclusively with income from my Social Security and a drawing from my holdings in gold and silver coin, which constantly grows in dollar value – as I always knew they would. Other than that, my retirement has allowed me the very deep pleasure of expanding my collections of U.S. and world coins and stamps, paid for from my reserve holdings, and through the sale of some collector's pieces that I no longer need nor want.

Epilogue

At this advanced stage of my life, my only real regret was selling my Florida house, and that I hadn't brought Scott and his family to join me there, instead of Pahrump. Yet the most comforting part of the "here and now" has actually been the secure establishment of my new family. Now at the age of 76, I find myself prone to doing what most people usually do at such an age – to look back with the usual questions – "Has it all been worth the effort?" "Suppose I'd made different choices?

Ron at home in Nevada, 2011

Would it have made any difference?" And again, as most reasonable people finally do, I come to the same conclusion: such contemplation yields nothing of worth. What is the past is fixed in time and space, and no amount of re-hashing will change an atom of it.

"The moving finger writes, and having writ, moves on. Nor all your piety nor wit shall lure it back to cancel half a line, nor all your tears wash out a word of it." (*The Rubáiyát of Omar Khayyám*, Edward FitzGerald)

I certainly cannot claim that all of my decisions were right, or that they even represented the best choices that I could have made. And yet, it is the composite of all of those decisions that has placed me in the very real circumstances of the "here and now." But, I can say one thing with honesty and certainty. I am comforted in the knowledge that I've made every effort during my lifetime to follow at least one tenant of the Hippocratic Oath: Do no harm.

But one final thought does remain. Among the blessings that have graced my life is the fact that I was fortunate enough to have drawn lucky on the genetic pool. My health still holds, and my capacity for ambitious dreams and hope remains undiminished. In short, if the fates are kind and the wind blows in the right direction, there may well be more thrilling adventures yet to come, before that last bell tolls.

We are no other than a moving row
of magic lantern shapes that come and go.
'Round with the sun-lumed lantern held
at midnight, by the master of the show.

We're naught but pieces of the game He plays
here upon this checkerboard of nights and days,
As hither and thither He moves – and checks – and slays
and one by one, back into the closet lays.

–*The Rubáiyát of Omar Khayyám*, by Edward FitzGerald

Made in the USA
Middletown, DE
05 April 2018